THE CAREGIVER'S GUIDE TO STRICT AND LOVING DISCIPLINE

The Tools You Need to Give a Spanking by the Book!

By Clarine Klein, Professor of Spankology

Copyright © 2022 Clarine Klein
All rights reserved.

ISBN: 979-8-9857980-0-5
Imprint: Studio Bebop Inc.

Cover Illustration and Additional Illustrations by Arkham-Insanity
https://www.patreon.com/isadoraarkham
https://twitter.com/ArkhamInsanity

Professor Sally Illustration by CourtJeStar

This book is a work of fiction. Activities represented in this book are fantasies only.

No part of this publication may be reproduced or transmitted in any form or by any means, electronic or mechanical, including photocopying, recording, or by any information storage or retrieval system, without permission in writing from the publisher. Anyone performing any unauthorized act in relation to this publication may be liable to criminal prosecution and civil claims for damages.

Before We Begin

Allow me to set aside the fun pseudo-academic façade for just a moment and state from the start that **this book is intended for adults engaging in <u>CONSENTING</u> ageplay, spanking, and other related kinks only!**

<u>NO CHILD SHOULD EVER BE HIT FOR DISCIPLINE</u>

I don't care if you grew up as a wooden spoon survivor, or were like me and just had a bone-deep interest in spanking since before you can remember. Unlike the tantalizing nonsense in this book, **actual** scientists have proven time and time again that corporal punishment does not work to improve behavior and is both harmful and abusive to those who receive it. To that end, allow me to clarify that this book is meant to be a parody of those god awful raising your kids the "right" way through old-fashioned Christian fundamentalism and spanking books (Looking at you Dare to Discipline, God, the Rod, and your Child's Bod, and all the dreck written by the Pearls), and as such it is not to be taken as any sort of endorsement of those sorts of parenting styles. Because, yeah. They're gross.

Finally, **all of the advice in this book is intended to be titillating and fun first and foremost.** Granted, I've done my best to keep things practical and based in reality whenever possible (after all, I really do have a lot of first-hand experience going over people's knees), but this book is still intended to be read with the implicit understanding that we're setting aside good and responsible kink practices in favor of exploring a fun fantasy world for a while. So, keeping that in mind, **if something sounds like fun and you've never tried it before, <u>PLEASE</u> do some additional research before you try it.**

All right, phew! Now that we've gotten all of that out of the way, let me slip back into my fancy professorial lab coat and let's begin our journey into the wonderful world of hyper-embarrassing, spank-normative discipline!

TABLE OF CONTENTS

Why Spanking? 1
    Are you sure spanking my Little or Middle is really the right idea? 1
    Wait a minute! Aren't I supposed to ground my Little or Middle? 1
    What is Effective Discipline? 2
    An Example of Effective Discipline in Action 2

Avoiding Common Mistakes 7
    A Caregiver Corrects Misbehavior, not Bad Behavior 7
    A Caregiver is Consistent 7
    A Caregiver Never Spanks in Anger 7
    A Caregiver Does Not Debate, They Declare 7
    A Caregiver Does Not Wait to Spank 8
    A Caregiver Knows That You Are Never Too Old for a Spanking! 8

Achieving Effective Discipline through Embarrassment 9

Achieving Effective Discipline Through Scolding 11
    The Purpose of Scolding 11
    How to Scold a Little or Middle the Correct Way 12

Achieving Effective Discipline Through Supplementary Punishments 15
    The Three Categories of Supplementary Punishment 15

Recommended Supplementary Punishments 19
    Corner Time 19
    Punishment Mats 21
    Early Bedtime 23
    Loss of Pants or Underwear Privileges 23
    Pubic Hair Removal 25
    Diapers and Pull-Ups 27
    Mouth Soaping 31
    Enemas 33
    Figging 37

The Five Types of Spanking 43
Disciplinary Spankings 43
Attitude Adjustment Spankings 43
Weekly Maintenance Spankings 47
Encouragement Spankings 49
Spankings for Emotional Release 51

Levels of Disobedience and the Severity Spectrum 57
Understanding the Severity Spectrum 57
Minor Misbehavior 57
Standard Misbehavior 58
Serious Misbehavior 58
Appropriately Categorizing Misbehavior 59

Selecting the Right Spanking Implement For Your Little or Middle 65
The Two Categories of Spanking Implement 65
The Two Types of Impact Sensation 65
Which Spanking Implement should I use? 66
A Brief Note on the Importance of Implement Storage 67

Recommended Spanking Implements 71
The Hand 71
The Wooden Spoon 73
The Hairbrush 75
The Bath Brush 79
The Paddle 81
The Slipper 83
The Belt 85
The Leather Strap 87
The Tawse 89
The Cane 91
The Switch 93

Selecting the Right Spanking Position for Your Little or Middle 99
What to Consider When Choosing a Spanking Position 99
Review What You've Learned 101

Recommended Spanking Positions 103
Over the Knee 103
Bending Over 107
Lying Facedown 109
The Diaper Position.. 111

Giving a Spanking the Correct Way 113
When Should a Spanking Take Place?.. 113
Where Should a Spanking Take Place? 114
A Proper Spanking is a Spanking on the Bare Bottom, Always! 115
Preparing Your Little or Middle for Their Spanking 116
Increasing Severity with Water, Baby Oil, and Capsaicin Cream 118
Where to Aim During a Spanking... 119
Crafting the Perfect Swat.. 120
How Long Should a Spanking Be?.. 121
Finishing a Spanking the Correct Way 122
Dealing With Uncooperative Littles and Middles......................................

Utilizing Behavior Contracts to Achieve Effective Discipline 129
Behavior Contracts are a Team Effort.. 129
Remember to Keep it Simple, Silly!.. 129
An Effective Contract is a Visible Contract.. 130
The Four Components of an Effective Behavior Contract....................... 130
Example Behavior Contract... 131

Achieving Effective Discipline via Delegation of Spanking Authority............. 137

Congratulations! 145

Answers to Frequently Asked Questions 149

Why Spanking?

In spite of leaps and bounds in both technology and society as a whole, there are still some truths that remain universal. The sky is blue, ice cream is delicious, and nothing adjusts a bratty attitude quite like a sound spanking.

While the latter is an immutable fact, sadly not all Caregivers are prepared to give the sort of no-nonsense discipline that their Little or Middle needs. To that end, it is the intention of this book is to condense over two decades of meticulous research in the field of Spankology in order to provide you, the Caregiver, with all of the information you will need to be able to give a spanking that is guaranteed to get results.

Are you sure spanking my Little or Middle is really the right idea?

Don't be silly, of course I am!

There's a reason why it's called "giving" someone a spanking. A spanking isn't just a punishment for misbehavior. A spanking is a gift a loving Caregiver gives their Little or Middle every time they stray past the boundaries set for them. It not only serves as a swift and effective consequence for bad behavior in the moment, but also as a valuable resource for your Little or Middle to draw upon when they are inevitably tempted to misbehave again in the future.

So, bearing that in mind, why wouldn't you choose spanking?

Wait a minute! Aren't I supposed to ground my Little or Middle?

Absolutely not!

Grounding is not only barbaric, but also completely ineffective at improving a Little or Middle's behavior, and therefore has no place in a modern Caregiver's disciplinary arsenal. Just ask yourself, would you rather spend the next week or more playing jailer to your Little or Middle, making the both of you increasingly miserable as resentment builds between you, or would you rather engage in a disciplinary strategy that has been proven time and time again by Spankologists around the world to actually produce positive results in the form of Effective Discipline?

Yeah. I thought so.

What is Effective Discipline?

In the field of Spankology, Effective Discipline is achieved when a Caregiver metes out a punishment or series of punishments that not only serve as a negative and unpleasant consequence for misbehavior in the moment, but also establishes an anchor point in the psyche of their Little or Middle that can be drawn upon as an internal deterrent toward repeated misbehavior in the future.

An Example of Effective Discipline in Action

I understand that to the layperson Caregiver, the concept of Effective Discipline can be intimidating, but allow me to assure you that it really isn't! With just a bit of training and the proper mindset, it's as easy as could be. Take for example, the following anecdote.

—

Rhen the Middle knows that her bedtime is at 10:30 every night when she has classes in the morning, and that she should be showered and in her pajamas by no later than 10:00. However, come 11, her Caregiver, Dana, finds her not only out of bed and playing games on her computer, but she hasn't even showered or changed into her pajamas yet!

Rhen may not realize it, but she is testing Dana as a Caregiver. Does she really mean what she says about having a bedtime and needing to be ready for bed, or is that just her making a suggestion? Well, she gets the answer to that question just as soon as Dana drags her over to her bed, yanks down her pants and panties, and puts her over her knee for a long, bare-bottomed spanking that leaves her sniffling and sleeping on her stomach.

—

In the above scenario, not only was Rhen punished for her misbehavior that night, but now the next time she is tempted to stay up past her bedtime she will be able to think back to what happened the last time she wasn't in bed by 10:30 and decide for herself that it's not worth the risk of a sore bottom.

Granted, not every lesson a Caregiver imparts to their Little or Middle through a sore bottom takes quite so quickly as it might for Rhen, but that's just fine. Bottoms are made for spanking (why else would they have evolved to be so soft and jiggly?), and you as a Caregiver should feel confident that eventually the lesson will sink in. Be it one spanking later or ten!

That's the power of Effective Discipline.

Review What You've Learned

Complete the quiz below to test what you've learned so far. The correct answers can be found by turning the page over, so do your best and no cheating!

1. A spanking is a gift a loving Caregiver gives their Little or Middle every time they stray past the boundaries set for them.

    a. True

    b. False

2. Grounding your Little or Middle is an appropriate punishment.

    a. True

    b. False

3. A spanking that achieves Effective Discipline only needs to be given once.

    a. True

    b. False

> Quiz Answers
> a. True
> b. False
> b. False

Avoiding Common Mistakes

Even the best of us make mistakes sometimes, and that's okay! That being said, there are a few things that you as a Caregiver should keep in mind when it comes to working toward achieving Effective Discipline with your Little or Middle. Many of these topics will be expanded upon further in later chapters of this book, but the short and sweet bullet points are as follows.

A Caregiver Corrects Misbehavior, not Bad Behavior.

No Little or Middle is ever "bad", and as such a Caregiver should never imply that they are by saying they are behaving "badly". Rather, when a Little or Middle isn't behaving the way they should be, then they are misbehaving. Misbehavior must be corrected, but Misbehavior is not an identity.

A Caregiver is Consistent

If something is a spankable offense, then it's a spankable offense always. Even when it might not be convenient to give your Little or Middle a spanking, you owe it to them to do so anyway.

A Caregiver Never Spanks in Anger

Remember, a spanking is something you give your Little or Middle, not inflict. As such, it should always be given with love and a clear head. If you need a moment to cool down, put them in the corner and take a walk!

A Caregiver Does Not Debate, They Declare

Despite what every Little or Middle around the world might think, they do not in fact know best. You, their Caregiver, do, and while it's important to listen to what your Little or Middle has to say, at the end of the day, you are the one in charge and they need to respect that. Therefore, when you say it's time for a spanking, it's time for a spanking, plain and simple.

A Caregiver Does Not Wait to Spank

Effective Discipline is discipline that is delivered as swiftly as possible, lest your Little or Middle develop an attitude of "I can misbehave now and figure out how to get out of my punishment later." To that end, the time between misbehavior and a spanking should be as short as possible. For instance, if your Little or Middle is acting up in the middle of the store, rather than waiting until you get home to spank them, take them into the restroom and warm their bottom for them before returning to your shopping. They may not like it, but they'll definitely think twice about misbehaving in public again!

A Caregiver Knows That You Are Never Too Old for a Spanking!

Despite what just about every Middle might have you believe, you are never too old for a spanking. If a Little or Middle is willing to misbehave, then they should be willing to face the consequences as well. Pure and simple.

Achieving Effective Discipline through Embarrassment

Effective Discipline starts long before the first swat of a spanking is ever given, and Embarrassment is the foundation upon which all memorable and behavior-improving consequences are built. Spankings are supposed to be embarrassing, it's one of their most valuable attributes, and when they are paired with Supplementary Punishments such as mouth soaping or being forced to wear a diaper or pull-up (topics which will be discussed further in the following chapter), you as the Caregiver are elevating what would otherwise be a mundane and forgettable series of consequences to the level of truly Effective Discipline which will stick with your Little or Middle long after their bottom has stopped smarting.

REMEMBER!

IF YOUR LITTLE OR MIDDLE IS WILLING TO ACT LIKE A CHILD, THEN YOU SHOULD HAVE NO PROBLEM TREATING THEM LIKE ONE!

ACHIEVING EFFECTIVE DISCIPLINE THROUGH SCOLDING

No spanking is ever given in silence, therefore mastering the art of scolding your Little or Middle the correct way is critical to achieving Effective Discipline.

The Purpose of Scolding

Scolding is a rhetorical device intended to help shepherd your Little or Middle toward an understanding of what they did wrong, why it was wrong, and how they should act in the future. To that end, when scolding your Little or Middle, never imply that they are intrinsically "bad", and avoid using any harsh "you are" statements such as "you are a bad girl!"

REMEMBER!
YOUR LITTLE OR MIDDLE IS NOT THEIR MISBEHAVIOR, AND THEY SHOULD NEVER BE MADE TO FEEL THAT WAY!

How to Scold a Little or Middle the Correct Way

Much as my contemporaries in the field of Spankology are loath to admit, scolding is more of an art than it is a science, and it is only through repetition and practice that a Caregiver is able to discover their own personal scolding style and hone their skills. That being said, it may help you as a Caregiver to think of scolding your Little or Middle as more of pre-disciplinary interview, instead of a one-sided lecture you dole out before they go across your lap.

To that end, rather than asking your Little or Middle basic yes or no questions such as "Do you understand that what you did was naughty?", you should instead pose open-ended question to them such as "Why was what you did naughty?" or "What should you have done instead?". Approaching your scolding from this angle will afford your Little or Middle the opportunity they need to reflect more fully on their misbehavior and to understand why it was wrong, thereby making them an active participant in their punishment in a way that will help you both to achieve Effective Discipline.

Some examples of effective questions a Caregiver can ask their Little or Middle while scolding them include:

- "Why are you up past your bedtime?"
- "When are you supposed to be in bed by?"
- "What are you going to do tomorrow night when it's time for bed?"

Review What You've Learned

Complete the quiz below to test what you've learned so far. The correct answers can be found by turning the page over, so do your best and no cheating!

1. The purpose of scolding a Little or Middle is to list out to them what they did wrong.

    a. True

    b. False

2. A Little or Middle should be told in no uncertain terms that they are bad when their Caregiver is scolding them.

    a. True

    b. False

3. A Caregiver should focus on asking yes or no questions while scolding their Little or Middle.

    a. True

    b. False

Quiz Answers
b. False
b. False
b. False

Achieving Effective Discipline Through Supplementary Punishments

It is important to note before we proceed any further that while routine and consistent spankings are incredibly important in achieving Effective Discipline with Littles and Middles, they should not be the only tool a Caregiver employs to correct misbehavior. Just as variety is the spice of life, a spanking paired with one or more Supplementary Punishments yields an even greater positive change in behavior than a spanking on its own.

The Three Categories of Supplementary Punishment

While there are a virtually endless number of potential Supplementary Punishments a Caregiver might use to enhance their Little or Middle's spankings, they all nevertheless fall into one of the three following categories.

Reflective Punishments

Punishments such as corner time, sitting on a punishment mat, or being sent to bed early all aim to provide a disobedient Little or Middle with the necessary time and headspace needed to reflect upon their misbehavior, why what they might have done was wrong, and how they can do better in the future so as to avoid being punished for the same thing again.

Humiliation Punishments

Humiliation Punishments such as loss of pants privileges or being required to wear diapers or pull-ups are punishments that do just that, humiliate your Little or Middle. Granted, that may sound cruel on the surface, but as we discussed in the previous chapter, Embarrassment is the foundation upon which all Effective Discipline is built. Therefore, just as a stitch in time saves nine, a healthy dose of embarrassment in the moment helps a Caregiver to avoid having to discipline their Little or Middle for the same thing again in the future.

Discomfort Punishments

Punishments such as mouth soaping, figging, or enemas all aim to prolong a disobedient Little or Middle's overall discomfort during a particular discipline session. Prolonging discomfort has been scientifically proven by Spankologists to exponentially increase a discipline session's memorability, therefore leading to overall improved behavior.

Review What You've Learned

Complete the quiz below to test what you've learned so far. The correct answers can be found by turning the page over, so do your best and no cheating!

1. A Spanking on its own is just as effective at achieving Effective Discipline as a spanking and a Supplementary Punishment.

    a. True

    b. False

2. Reflective Punishments involve a mirror so your Little or Middle can see how red their bottom is.

    a. True

    b. False

3. There are _____ categories of Supplementary Punishments.

    a. 1

    b. 2

    c. 3

    d. 1,000

Quiz Answers!
b. False
b. False
c. 3

Recommended Supplementary Punishments

Outlined below are a list of recommended Supplementary Punishments that have been thoroughly tested by this author and are guaranteed to achieve Effective Discipline with any Little or Middle when utilized correctly.

Corner Time

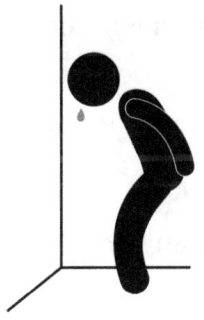

Requiring a Little or Middle to stand facing the corner is the quintessential Reflective Punishment, and should be made use of liberally. Corner time is a fantastic tool both for before a spanking is given as a means for a Little or Middle to reflect on what they've done and the consequences they are about to receive, as well as after a spanking as a means for a Little or Middle to gradually calm down and reflect on how they should behave moving forward.

Utilizing Corner Time the Correct Way

Step 1. Select a suitable corner for your Little or Middle to stand in for the duration of their Corner Time. If a suitable corner is not available, an open stretch of wall will work just as well.

Step 2. *(Optional)* If this particular instance of Corner Time is taking place before a spanking, bare your Little or Middle's bottom.

Step 3. Instruct your Little or Middle to lean forward and push their nose as far as they can into the corner. If possible, the tip of their nose should touch the intersection between the two walls in front of them.

Alternatively, if your Little or Middle is facing a wall, have them hold either a coin or a piece of paper in place against said wall using the tip of their nose instead.

Step 4. Instruct your Little or Middle to either interlock their fingers on top of their head, or else fold their arms behind their back. Doing so, along with the measures taken in Step 3, will ensure that they remain in place for the duration of their Corner Time with the minimum amount of squirming.

Step 5. Inform your Little or Middle that they will remain in that exact position until you say otherwise.

If they then proceed to break position after this warning, deliver 6 - 12 swats to their bottom and warm them that if it happens again they can expect to receive an additional spanking along with any additional Supplementary Punishments you may deem appropriate come bedtime that evening.

Step 6. Leave your Little or Middle to reflect in the corner for anywhere between five minutes to half an hour, and then proceed with the remainder of their punishment.

Punishment Mats

Requiring your Little or Middle to sit on a Punishment Mat is an excellent way to keep their bottom smarting long after their spanking is over while they have a time out, write an apology letter, or catch up on homework they might have missed.

Picking the Right Punishment Mat for Your Little or Middle

While a Punishment Mat can certainly be intimidating to any Little or Middle required to sit on one, purchasing one as a Caregiver doesn't have to be. Any sort of broad base with evenly-spaced, stiff bristles or plastic "spikes" is all you need. To that end, outlined below are three potential options a Caregiver might use as a Punishment Mat, all of which this author has conducted extensive first-hand research on and can confirm are more than capable of getting your point across without breaking the bank.

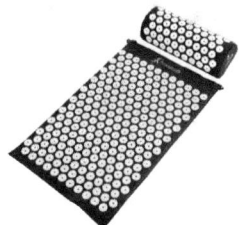

Acupressure Mat

Pros:

- Inexpensive
- Perfect size and shape
- Excellent density of blunted points
- The accompanying neck pillow can be utilized to discipline more sensitive areas of a Little or Middle by making them spread their bottom cheeks and straddle it

Cons:

- Can be a little too intense for some Littles or Middles
- Sometimes hard to find in stock online

Welcome Mat

Pros:

- Denser concentration of shorter spikes make it easier to sit on than an Acupressure Mat

Cons:

- Doesn't necessarily convey a "discipline" aesthetic, although calling it an "unwelcome mat" is always fun.
- May need to be cut down to shape before it can be used

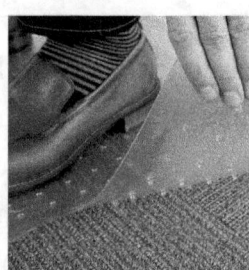

Office Chair Mat

Pros:

- Shorter Spikes are more gentle on sensitive Littles and Middles

Cons:

- Expensive
- Needs to be cut down to shape before it can be used

Early Bedtime

Being sent to bed early is a tried and true Reflective Punishment, especially for bratty Middles. There are very few things that will grind the gears of a disobedient brat quite like having to lie on their tummy due to a sore bottom as they attempt to will themselves to sleep while their friends are able to stay up and play.

Note: While a Little or Middle may certainly benefit from being sent to bed early, that does not mean they should ever be sent to bed on an empty stomach. It is your responsibility as a Caregiver to ensure that your Little or Middle is always getting the nutrition they need to stay healthy and strong, which includes a proper dinner. Always.

Loss of Pants or Underwear Privileges

Rescinding your Little or Middle's ability to wear pants, shorts, a skirt, etc. (as well as potentially their underwear or panties too) is an incredibly simple but devastatingly effective Humiliation Punishment, especially for Middles. Not only is it incredibly embarrassing, it also makes it impossible for your Little or Middle to hide a well-spanked bottom. Plus, it leaves them perfectly prepared for any subsequent spankings you may wish to give them!

Pubic Hair Removal

Shaving a Little or Middle's pubic hair is a simple yet extremely effective way of not only embarrassing them, but also serves as an excellent means of facilitating the proper headspace for them to understand that you are the one in charge, not them. Especially for Middles.

Note: It is this author's strong recommendation that all Caregivers require their Little or Middle to maintain a cleanly shaven pubic area at all times for the exact same reasons as stated above for why it makes such an excellent Supplementary Punishment.

What You'll Need

- An electric hair trimmer
- A bath towel
- A hand towel
- A bowl of warm water
- Shaving cream (ideally something tingly)
- A fresh multi-blade razor
- *(Optional)* A gentle depilatory cream

Utilizing Proper Technique

Step 1. Lay out your bath towel on top of your Little or Middle's bed.

Step 2. Strip your Little or Middle naked if they not already and direct them to lie down on their back atop the bath towel you laid out in **Step 1** with their hands pillowed behind their head.

Step 3. Explain to your Little or Middle that their hands are to remain exactly where they are until you are finished shaving their pubic area. Warn them that if they do not cooperate, you will give them a spanking, and / or require them to wear a diaper or pull-up for the next week.

Step 4. Spread your Little or Middle's legs wide enough to fully expose their genitals.

Step 5. Using your electric hair trimmer, clear away your Little or Middle's pubic hair until only stubble remains.

Step 6. Wet your hand towel in your bowl of water and wipe down your Little or Middle's pubic area.

Step 7. Spread a generous amount of shaving cream over your Little or Middle's genitals and pubic area.

Step 8. Using a fresh multi-blade razor, shave away the remainder of your Little or Middle's pubic hair.

Step 9. Once again wet your hand towel in your bowl of water and wipe away any remaining shaving cream and loose hair follicles.

Step 10. Repeat **Steps 7 - 9** until all pubic hair has been removed.

Step 11. *(Optional)* Following the instructions for the depilatory cream you have chosen, spread it over your Little or Middle's pubic area, allowing it to sit for as long as is obstructed, before repeating **Step 9** one final time.

Step 12. Tell your Little or Middle how adorable they look, and then help them sit up and allow them to explore their new haircut.

Diapers and Pull-Ups

Particularly effective with Middles who have become "too big for their britches", requiring your Little or Middle to wear diapers or pull-ups in lieu of their usual underwear or panties is one of the most embarrassing Supplementary Punishments a Caregiver has at their disposal.

Note: While this particular subsection is dedicated specifically to the practice of requiring your Little or Middle to wear a diaper or pull-up, it should be noted that this punishment can be enhanced to great effect by also requiring your Little or Middle to wear a onesie as well.

Utilizing Proper Technique

Step 1. Decide how long you intend to require your Little or Middle to wear diapers or pull-ups for. This author recommends that Caregivers utilize this particular Supplementary Punishment in one-week increments.

Step 2. Decide whether or not you will require your Little or Middle to "use" their diapers or pull-ups, or if they may continue to make use of the bathroom as usual.

Step 3. Inform your Little or Middle exactly how long you intend for them to be required to wear diapers or pull-ups for along with whether or not they will be allowed to use the bathroom as usual during this punishment.

Step 4. *(Optional)* Confiscate all of your Little or Middle's "normal" underwear or panties so that they will not be tempted to attempt to sidestep their punishment.

Step 5. Bare your Little or Middle's bottom like you would normally for a spanking, and then help them into their first diaper or pull-up. Don't forget the baby powder!

Step 6. Once their new diaper or pull-up is securely in place, help your Little or Middle redress (assuming you are not rescinding their pants privileges as well) and inform them in no uncertain terms that the only time that diaper or pull-up will be coming off is when you change them into a new one every morning (or as necessary).

Step 7. Regardless of whether or not your Little or Middle is allowed to use the bathroom as normal, for the duration of their punishment, make a point of checking their diaper or pull-up when they wake up in the morning, before they go to bed at night, and occasionally throughout the day as well. Do so by asking them outright if they are wearing their diaper or pull-up, as well as whether they need to be changed. If your Little or Middle informs you that they do not need to be charged, proceed to confirm this fact for yourself by pulling back the waistband of their shorts or pant, or else lifting up their skirt or dress.

REMEMBER!

EMBARRASSMENT IS THE END GOAL OF THIS PUNISHMENT, SO DON'T BE SHY ABOUT LETTING OTHERS FIND OUT YOUR LITTLE OR MIDDLE IS WEARING A DIAPER OR PULL-UP!

Recommended Brands of Diapers and Pull-Ups

For many Littles and Middles (such as this author, though she is loath to admit she has ever been subjected to such an indignity it must be noted with all vehemence), "traditional" brands of diapers and pull-ups / training pants are simply too small, and while one could simply purchase their adult equivalents from any grocery store or pharmacy, those options tend not to adhere well to the Little / Middle aesthetic and headspace. Worry not, though, dear reader, the following is a non-comprehensive list of recommended brands of both diapers and pull-ups that will not only fit any Little or Middle, but will also look the part too!

Brand	Type
Tykables Unicorns Diapers	Diaper
Tykables Little Rawrs Diapers	Diaper
ABU Little Kings	Diaper
ABU BunnyHopps 2-Tape	Diaper
Rearz Barnyard Elite Adult Diapers	Diaper

Brand	Type
Rearz Safari Nighttime Briefs	Diaper
Rearz Princess Pink Overnight Briefs	Diaper
Rearz Lil' Monsters Diapers	Diaper
Rearz Rebel Incontinence Briefs	Diaper
Mermaid Tales All-Night Briefs	Diaper
Felicity Super Absorbent Underwear	Pull-Up
Goodnites XL Nighttime Bedwetting Underwear	Pull-Up

Mouth Soaping

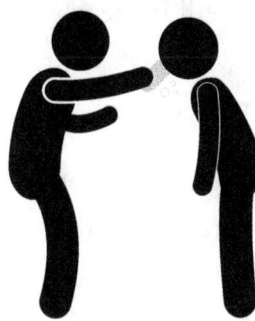
Washing out the mouth of a Little or Middle with a bar of soap is an excellent punishment for lying, swearing, and even talking back. A proper mouth soaping takes less than five minutes to properly execute, but will have a positive effect on the behavior of your Little or Middle for hours to come!

Utilizing Proper Technique

Step 1. Select a bar of plain, unscented soap such as Ivory or Dial.

Step 2. Holding the bar of soap under warm running water, rotate it between your palms until any hard corners or edges have been rounded over and the bar of soap has developed thorough coating of lather.

Step 3. Shut off the flow of water and order your Little or Middle to come stand in front of you.

Step 4. Explain to your Little or Middle that you expect them to cooperate with their mouth soaping, and that if they try to resist it, you will have no problem spanking them before they go to bed that evening.

Step 5. With the hand you are not currently holding the soap in, gently but firmly grasp your Little or Middle by the back of their neck to help them stay still during the following steps.

Step 6. Direct your Little or Middle to open their mouth nice and wide, again reminding them that failure to comply will mean a spanking before bedtime that evening if necessary.

Step 7. Proceed to wash out the inside of your Little or Middle's mouth by first scrubbing the bar of soap across the top of their tongue. Follow this up by working the bar of soap along the insides of their cheeks.

Step 8.   *(Optional)* Rasp the bar of along your Little or Middle's top and bottom molars. Doing so will lodge small pieces of soap into them, greatly enhancing the severity of the punishment as it will be nearly impossible to remove all of them during **Step 11** and will leave your Little or Middle tasting soap long after their punishment is over.

Step 9.   Instruct your Little or Middle to bite down onto the bar of soap before letting it go. Inform them that you expect it to remain right where it is until you give them permission to spit it out.

Step 10.   Place your Little or Middle into the corner for up to, but no longer than, five minutes.

Note: Soap is caustic and can start to burn your Little or Middle's tongue if left there for too long. So, make sure to instruct them to spit it out immediately if they begin to feel any sort of burning sensation inside their mouth.

Step 11.   Finally, release your Little or Middle from their corner time and allow them to rinse their mouth out with water.

Enemas

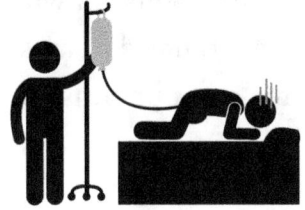

While the actual medical benefits of flushing out one's colon are murky at best, it cannot be denied that giving a Little or Middle an enema as a Supplementary Punishment is both humiliating and extremely effective at encouraging better behavior in the future.

Utilizing Proper Technique

Step 1.   Purchase a 1 Quart enema bag kit either from an online retailer or your local pharmacy.

Note: Smaller enema "bulbs" and pre-filled options are available for purchase as well, but this author highly recommends sticking with the tried and true enema bag when it comes to giving your Little or Middle a punishment enema.

Step 2.   Bare your Little or Middle's bottom and put them into the corner for a time out while you prepare their enema.

Step 3.   Ensure that the nozzle at the end of the hose protruding from the enema bag has been cinched off to prevent any potential leakage and then begin to fill the enema bag with water that is approximately body temperature.

Note: Do not attempt to deviate from the temperature specified in this step. Water that is too hot or too cold will cause extremely unpleasant cramping that will disrupt your Little or Middle's headspace and eliminate any potential for Effective Discipline to be achieved.

Step 4. While the enema bag is filling, hold a bar of unscented soap (such as Ivory or Dial) just below the stream of water as it reaches the top of the bag. Doing so will produce a warm and soapy enema solution with exactly the right ratio of soap to water that will be guaranteed to make your Little or Middle's upcoming punishment enema extra unpleasant without being too harsh.

Step 5. Once the enema bag has been fully filled to its 1 quart capacity, shut off the flow of water and hang it up somewhere that is slightly above eye level. The knobs on kitchen cabinets or the shower rod in a bathroom are both excellent options.

Step 6. Uncoil the length of hosing attached to the base of the enema bag and coax out any trapped air bubbles by gently tapping its sides and unclamping the nozzle at the end of the hose long enough to release them.

Step 7. Call your Little or Middle over to stand beside you and direct them to spread their legs a shoulders' width apart and either bend over a nearby table or countertop, or else bend over and grab their knees. Alternatively, you may instruct them to take up a position on their hands and knees with their bottom elevated.

Step 8. Using the fingers of your non-dominant hand, spread the bottom cheeks of your Little or Middle as wide as they will go, fully exposing their anus. Then, using the bar of soap from **Step 4**, lubricate their anus using anywhere from 1 - 3 fingers.

Note: Humiliation is a core component of this punishment, so do not rush! Take your time and let your Little or Middle bask in their embarrassment before you move on to the next step.

Step 9. Release your Little or Middle's bottom cheeks and use the bar of soap from **Step 4** to lubricate the nozzle at the end of the enema bag's hose.

Step 10. Once the enema nozzle and your Little or Middle have both been thoroughly lubricated, once again spread their bottom cheeks using the fingers of your non-dominant hand and fully insert the enema nozzle into their anus.

Note: Enema nozzles are designed to be slim and painless when inserted. If you wish for the experience to be more uncomfortable for your Little or Middle, consider purchasing an aftermarket nozzle that has a greater diameter.

Step 11. Inform your Little or Middle that you are about to let go of the enema nozzle and that you expect them to hold it in place for the duration of their punishment.

Note: If for whatever reason your Little or Middle is having difficulty holding the enema nozzle in place themselves, it is fine to do it for them.

Step 12. With the nozzle securely in place, open its valve and allow gravity to take care of flowing the enema solution prepared in **Step 3** into your Little or Middle.

Step 13. Once the enema bag has been fully drained, close off the valve of the enema nozzle.

Step 14. *(Optional)* If you wish to further enhance the severty of this particular punishment, take this opportunity to repeat **Steps 3 - 13** once again.

Note: This technique is only for those Little or Middles who are experienced at taking punishment enemas, and you should never exceed two quarts during any punishment enema.

Step 15. Inform your Little or Middle that you are about to remove the enema nozzle from their bottom and that you expect them to hold in every last drop they've just taken in.

Note: If you wish to further enhance the embarrassment of this punishment for a Middle, ask them if they would like you to bring them a diaper or pull-up to "help" them out just in case.

Step 16. Once your Little or Miss is prepared, slowly remove the enema nozzle from their anus and tuck it into the top of the now drained enema bag for safe keeping.

Step 17. *(Optional)* Place your Little or Middle into corner time for anywhere from five to ten minutes.

Step 18. Allow your Little or Middle to run (well, speedwalk, I guarantee running will be the last thing on their mind) to the bathroom so that they may relieve themselves in private.

Figging

Dating back to as early as the Middle Ages when unscrupulous horse merchants would attempt to trick a potential buyer into believing an older horse was younger than it actually was, the act of figging in the context of Supplementary Punishments is the process of peeling a ginger root (or lubricating an appropriately-sized anal plug with diluted peppermint oil) and then inserting it into the anus of your disobedient Little or Middle. Not only is it incredibly embarrassing, but it is 100% guaranteed to stop a Little or Middle's sass right in its tracks!

How to Fig Your Little or Middle the Traditional Way Using Ginger

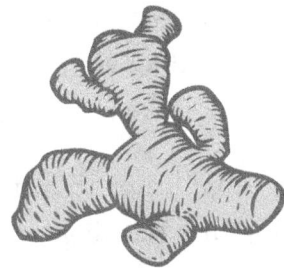

Step 1. Bare your Little or Middle's bottom and place them into the corner for a time out while you prepare the ginger root.

Step 2. Select a ginger root of appropriate size and shape that can be pared down into a plug around the length of your index finger and 1.5x - 2x as wide.

Step 3. Using a sharp knife, cut away the piece of ginger root you wish to carve into a plug from the rest of the root and proceed to peel away its outer skin, gradually shaping it into a basic plug shape with a rounded tip on one end and either a hooked or flared base to prevent it from slipping all the way inside of your Little or Middle on the other.

Step 4. Once the ginger root has been shaped to your satisfaction, call your Little or Middle over to stand beside you and direct them to spread their legs a shoulders' width apart and either bend over a nearby table or countertop, or else bend over and grab their knees. Alternatively, you may instruct them to take up a position on their hands and knees with their bottom elevated.

Step 5. While holding the peeled and prepared ginger root in your dominant hand, use the fingers of your free hand to spread the bottom cheeks of your Little or Middle as wide as they will go, fully exposing their anus.

Step 6. Instruct your Little or Middle to relax their bottom, and begin to gently but firmly push the prepared ginger root into their anus, making sure to twist it back and for as you do so to ensure an even coating of ginger oil along the outer rim and inside of your Little or Middle's anus.

Note: Humiliation is a core component of this punishment, so do not rush! Take your time and let your Little or Middle bask in their embarrassment before you move on to the next step.

Step 7. Your Little or Middle should start to feel a warm tingling sensation at this point, confirming that the ginger oil is doing its job. Continue to work the ginger root further and further inside of your Little or Middle until only it's hooked or flared base is left sticking out of them.

Step 8.   Release your Little or Middle's bottom cheeks and either return them back to the corner for a time out for anywhere from fifteen to thirty minutes, or else allow them to redress and go along their way with strict orders not to remove the ginger root until given permission to do so.

Over the course of the next ten to fifteen minutes, the warm tingling sensation inside of your Little or Middle's rectum and anus will rapidly increase into a distressing burning sensation, before then gradually fading back to normal over the course of another ten minutes.

Note: For maximum effect, do not remove the plug from your Little or Middle until at least half an hour has passed.

How to Fig Your Little or Middle Using an Anal Plug

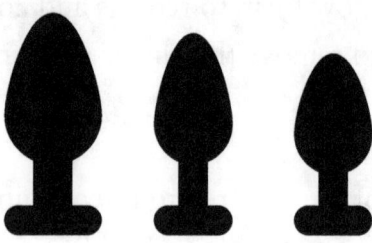

For some Caregivers, Littles, and Middles, the traditional ginger method of figging just isn't an option due to either personal preference or lack of availability. In cases such as these, swapping out a freshly peeled ginger root for a standard anal plug and diluted peppermint oil is just as effective!

Step 1. Bare your Little or Middle's bottom and place them into the corner for a time out while you prepare their plug.

Step 2. Select an anal plug that can be (relatively) comfortably worn for at least thirty minutes by your Little or Middle.

Step 3. Pour a generous portion of water-based lubricant into a small glass, add 3 - 10 drops of concentrated peppermint oil to it, and mix thoroughly occasionally dabbing some along the inside of your wrist to gauge its potency.

Step 4. Coat the plug you chose in **Step 2** with the lubricant prepared in **Step 3**.

Step 5. Call your Little or Middle over to stand beside you and direct them to spread their legs a shoulders' width apart and either bend over a nearby table or countertop, or else bend over and grab their knees. Alternatively, you may instruct them to take up a position on their hands and knees with their bottom elevated.

Step 6. While holding the lubricated plug in your dominant hand, use the fingers of your free hand to spread the bottom cheeks of your Little or Middle as wide as they will go, fully exposing their anus.

Step 7. Instruct your Little or Middle to relax their bottom, and begin to gently but firmly push the plug into their anus, making sure to twist it back and forth as you do so in order to ensure an even coating of diluted peppermint oil across the outer rim and inside of your Little or Middle's anus.

Note: Humiliation is a core component of this punishment, so do not rush! Take your time and let your Little or Middle bask in their embarrassment before you move on to the next step.

Step 8. Your Little or Middle should start to feel a cool tingling sensation at this point, confirming that the peppermint oil is doing its job. Continue to work the plug further into your Little or Middle until it is fully seated.

Step 9. Release your Little or Middle's bottom cheeks and either return them back to the corner for a time out for anywhere from fifteen to thirty minutes, or else allow them to redress and go along their way with strict orders not to remove the plug until given permission to do so.

Over the course of the next ten to fifteen minutes, the cool tingling sensation inside of your Little or Middle's rectum and anus will rapidly increase into a distressing burning sensation, before then gradually beginning to fade back to normal over the course of another ten minutes.

Note: For maximum effect, do not remove the plug from your Little or Middle until at least half an hour has passed.

The Five Types of Spanking

It is a woefully common misconception among Caregivers that the act of spanking a Little or Middle is a purely punitive exercise. In truth, there are actually five unique scenarios wherein a spanking may be utilized to great effect with a Little or Middle, and understanding what those scenarios are and how best to tailor your approach for each is the key to achieving *Effective Discipline. In the chapter Giving a Spanking the Correct Way* we will delve deeper into the specific mechanics of how to give a spanking the correct way, but for now let us examine the basics of each Spanking Type and when and how they should be utilized for your particular Little or Middle.

Disciplinary Spankings

Undoubtedly the most common form of spanking, Disciplinary Spankings are just that: spankings for discipline. When your Little or Middle's behavior is in need of correction, it's time for a Disciplinary Spanking!

Attitude Adjustment Spankings

At first blush, Attitude Adjustment Spankings and Disciplinary Spankings may seem interchangeable, but they absolutely are not! While Disciplinary Spankings are critical to ensuring that your Little or Middle reflects on their past misbehavior and resolves to behave better in the future, an Attitude Adjustment Spanking is a preventative measure intended to head off the need for a Disciplinary Spanking in the first place with a short sharp shock that will interrupt a Little or Middle's behavioral patterns enough to sufficiently adjust their attitude toward a more positive trajectory.

How to Give an Attitude Adjustment Spanking the Correct Way

Step 1. Immobilize your Little or Middle by taking hold of them by their upper arm, or bending them over and wrapping an arm around their waist.

Note: One of the key factors to interrupting your Little or Middle's current behavioral pattern is Embarrassment, therefore the more public the setting for their Attitude Adjustment Spanking, the better!

Step 2. Expose your Little or Middle's underwear or panties by either lowering their pants or shorts, or else raising the back of their skirt or dress.

Note: If your Little or Middle is currently wearing a diaper or pull-up, leave it where it is. While the extra padding will absorb the impact force of your swats in the following step, the noise of said padding crinkling will sting their pride just as much as a swat to their bottom would.

Step 3. Making sure to keep your palm rigid and your fingers and thumb pressed firmly together, deliver a dozen full-force swats to your Little or Middle's bottom, alternating cheeks with each swat.

Step 4. While keeping your Little or Middle held in position, ask them if they are going to start behaving themselves moving forward.

Note: If the answer to this question is not "yes", either repeat Step 3 or escalate to a Disciplinary Spanking.

Step 5. Restore your Little or Middle's clothing to where it was originally and let them go with one final admonition to behave themselves moving forward, before telling them that you love them and then giving them a hug and a kiss.

A Practical Example of an Attitude Adjustment Spanking in Action

Rhen the Middle is out with her Caregiver, Dana, shopping for groceries. Unfortunately, she would much rather be at home playing video games, and as a result, she is being extremely snappish with Dana, making their shopping trip unpleasant for the both of them. Her behavior has not quite reached the level where a proper Disciplinary Spanking would be called for, but if things continue as they are, it is just a matter of time before it will. Therefore, in order to head off that eventuality, Dana decides it's time to give her Middle a quick Attitude Adjustment Spanking there in the breakfast cereal aisle.

Thus decided, Dana bends Rhen over at the waist and pulls her in firmly against her hip, ensuring that she will not be able to wriggle free. She then proceeds to raise the back of her skirt, exposing the seat of her panties to the other customers around them. Then, while Rhen protests that she did not mean what she said and that she will be good, Dana proceeds to give her twelve full-armed swats to her bottom, making sure to alternate cheeks with each swat.

Dana then calmly asks Rhen if she is going to continue behaving like a brat, or if she's ready to start acting the way she knows she should. Rhen quickly assures her that she will be an angel from that point moving forward, and with a brief chuckle and a knowing look shared with those customers who just witnessed her Attitude Adjustment Spanking, Dana smooths Rhen's skirt back down into place and helps her to stand back up before giving her a firm hug and a kiss.

Rhen is of course incredibly embarrassed by this experience, but this combination of embarrassment and concentrated heat in her backside is enough to interrupt her pattern of behavior enough to realize that she was being a total brat and she resolves to be better. As a result, she and Dana are able to enjoy a nice time shopping together, before then deciding to go on a spur of the moment dinner date. All of which would not have been possible had Rhen continued to misbehave.

Weekly Maintenance Spankings

Similar to Attitude Adjustment Spankings, Maintenance Spankings are an invaluable tool for Caregivers to head off serious misbehavior before it has a chance to happen. For many Littles and Middles, a weekly trip over their Caregiver's knee for a mild Disciplinary Spanking is just the thing they need to help them to remember to behave themselves during the upcoming week, so be sure you don't forget them!

How to Give a Maintenance Spanking the Correct Way

Step 1. Choose a specific day and time that you will give your Little or Middle their weekly Maintenance Spanking.

Remember: Consistency is one of the key components of Effective Discipline, so make sure the time you pick is one you can stick to every week.

Step 2. Sit down with your Little or Middle at the appointed time decided upon in **Step 1** and discuss with them their behavior over the last week. Be sure to highlight things you were pleased with, as well as those areas where they might need improvement.

Step 3. Retrieve whatever Spanking Implement you may require, and then proceed to bare your Little or Middle's bottom and position them as you would for a Disciplinary Spanking.

Step 4. Remind your Little or Middle one more time that you are proud of them, but that you expect them to do better in the future and that you know this will help them do that..

Step 5. Proceed to give your Little or Middle a mild Disciplinary Spanking.

Step 6. After your Little or Middle has calmed down enough to talk, sit them on your lap and repeat what you discussed with them in **Step 2**.

Encouragement Spankings

Spankings for encouragement rather than punishment can often be an invaluable tool for those Caregivers whose Little or Middle has a habit of not fully applying themselves when it comes to their studies or other tasks.

How to Give an Encouragement Spanking the Correct Way

Step 1. Congratulate your Little or Middle for doing as well as they did with whatever it is they need encouragement to do better with.

Step 2. Explain that while you are happy they did as well as they did, you and your Little or Middle both know that they are capable of doing much better.

Note: Make sure you are both specific and encouraging in your admonition of your Little or Middle. Rather than simply saying "we both know you can do better in math class", say "We both know that you are very clever and are fully capable of bringing home an A+ if you apply yourself, don't we?"

Step 3. Explain to your Little or Middle that you are going to spank them now as a means of encouraging them to do better moving forward.

Step 4. Retrieve whatever Spanking Implement you may require, and then proceed to bare your Little or Middle's bottom and position them as you would for a Disciplinary Spanking.

Step 5. Remind your Little or Middle one more time that you are proud of them.

Step 6. Proceed to give your Little or Middle a Disciplinary Spanking.

Step 7. After your Little or Middle has calmed down enough to talk, sit them on your lap and repeat what you discussed with them in **Step 2**.

Step 8. Give your Little or Middle a big hug and a kiss and tell them that you love them.

An Example of When an Encouragement Spanking Should be Utilized

Rhen is a bright and gifted student, but she tends to slack off in her studies if left to her own devices. As a result, she brings home a midterm with a B+. While that is certainly a passing grade, her Caregiver, Dana, knows that it is still well below what she is capable of achieving when she applies herself. Therefore, in order to help encourage Rhen to do better in moving forward, Dana congratulates her on a job well done, and then takes her over her knee, bares her bottom, and proceeds to deliver a Disciplinary Spanking. After she is through spanking Rhen, her Dana then has her sit down on her lap and the two of them cuddle and discuss in greater detail both how and why Rhen can do better moving forward before then sharing a brief hug and a kiss.

Spankings for Emotional Release

Not all spankings need be for discipline or encouragement. Sometimes, your Little or Middle simply needs an opportunity to let go of whatever stress or anxiety has built up inside of them, and a spanking provides a safe and effective avenue for them to vent. Sure, they'll be sobbing and won't be able to sit down afterward, but that's the point!

How to Give a Spanking for Emotional Release the Correct Way

Step 1. Sit down with your Little or Middle and ask them what is bothering them. Spend however long it takes talking it out with your Little or Middle until they have gotten everything off of their chest. Then, if they are looking for solutions and not just an opportunity to vent, discuss with them potential ways they can avoid becoming this anxious and/or agitated again in the future.

Step 2. Inform your Little or Middle that you feel as their Caregiver that what they need right then is a chance to properly cry and release their pent up emotions, and that you are going to give them a spanking to help them do just that.

Step 3. Retrieve whatever Spanking Implement you may require, and then proceed to bare your Little or Middle's bottom and position them as you would for a Disciplinary Spanking.

Step 4. Remind your Little or Middle one more time that you are proud of them and that you love them.

Step 5. Proceed to spank your Little or Middle for as long as you feel is necessary for them to fully let go of any and all pent up anxiety and stress they might be carrying.

Note: For some Littles and Middles this means sobbing, but for others it may be only a few sniffles, so make sure you're paying attention!

Step 6. After your Little or Middle has calmed down enough to talk, sit them on your lap and remind them that they are loved and that you are here for them.

Step 7. Continue to hold your Little or Middle for as long as it takes for them to fully calm down and reach a state of total relaxation, and then give them a kiss and a hug and tell them once again that you love them.

Step 8. Your Little or Middle will be emotionally exhausted by this point (as well as physically, no doubt), so tuck them into bed and allow them to rest as long as they might need.

The Caregiver's Guide to Strict and Loving Discipline   53

> **Review What You've Learned**

Complete the quiz below to test what you've learned so far. The correct answers can be found by turning the page over, so do your best and no cheating!

1. There are _____ types of spankings.

    a. 1

    b. 2

    c. 3

    d. 4

    e. 5

2. Attitude Adjustment Spankings are given to correct misbehavior after it has happened.

    a. True

    b. False

3. It does not matter what day and time a weekly Maintenance Spanking is given.

    a. True

    b. False

> Quiz Answers
> e. 5
> b. False
> b. False

> **Put It Into Action!**

1) Using the information in this chapter, write down a scenario you witnessed this last week wherein one of the Five Types of Spankings would be applicable.

2) During the upcoming week, find an opportunity to give your Little or Middle an Attitude Adjustment Spanking.

3) Decide on a day and time that you will give your Little or Middle a Maintenance Spanking every week moving forward.

Levels of Disobedience and the Severity Spectrum

Just as not all spankings are the same, no two instances of misbehavior are entirely the same either. Bearing that in mind, it is important then as a Caregiver that you have a firm grasp of The Severity Spectrum so that the spankings you give to your Little or Middle will always be exactly what they need to help them behave better in the future.

Understanding the Severity Spectrum

The Severity Spectrum is comprised of three gradually increasing levels of severity.

The Severity Spectrum

Minor Misbehavior

Minor Misbehavior should be addressed with a Disciplinary Spanking or Attitude Adjustment Spanking.

Common examples of Minor Misbehavior may include:

- Talking back
- Having a bad attitude
- Having a messy room or play area
- Telling small fibs
- Not brushing teeth or washing hands
- Not staying hydrated

Standard Misbehavior

Standard Misbehavior should be addressed with a Disciplinary Spanking, as well as at least one Supplementary Punishment.

Common examples of Standard Misbehavior may include:

- Skipping lunch or dinner
- Staying up past bedtime
- Not finishing chores
- Not doing homework before playing
- Throwing a tantrum
- Swearing
- Telling lies
- Underperforming in classes

Serious Misbehavior

When possible, rather than addressing Serious Misbehavior as one single instance of misbehavior, it instead should be broken down into individual offenses (staying up past bedtime, sneaking out of the house, drinking alcohol, etc.) and addressed over multiple punishments.

Common examples of Serious Misbehavior may include:

- Not taking medication
- Sneaking out of the house
- Drinking alcohol
- Direct defiance or disobedience
- Failing a class or test

Appropriately Categorizing Misbehavior

Where exactly an offense falls on The Severity Spectrum is entirely dependent on both the standards of the Caregiver in question and the disposition of their Little or Middle. For some Caregivers, staying up past your bedtime is considered Serious Misbehavior, while for others strict adherence to bedtimes is less important and as such only counts as Standard or even Minor Misbehavior. Therefore, it is important not to approach dealing with the misbehavior of your Little or Middle with a "one size fits all" approach. By that same token, however, it is also important not to fall into the trap of becoming too granular in your approach to The Severity Spectrum.

REMEMBER!

MISBEHAVIOR IS MISBEHAVIOR, PURE AND SIMPLE!

Above all else, discipline should be intuitive, not some overly thought out series of equations with multiple factors and moving parts to determine the exact number of swats your Little or Middle deserves. When in doubt, always err on the side of strictness. As we discussed in the chapter Why Spanking?, bottoms are meant to be spanked, and you can rest assured that no Little or Middle has ever not needed their attitude adjusted at least a little bit and a sore bottom is never not helpful in curbing potential misbehavior.

Review What You've Learned

Complete the quiz below to test what you've learned so far. The correct answers can be found by turning the page over, so do your best and no cheating!

1. All misbehavior is the same.

    a. True

    b. False

2. All Caregivers should categorize misbehavior the same on the Severity Spectrum.

    a. True

    b. False

3. When possible, rather than addressing Serious Misbehavior as one single instance of misbehavior, it instead should be broken down into individual offenses and addressed over multiple punishments.

    a. True

    b. False

Quiz Answers
b. False
b. False
a. True

Put It Into Action!

Using the information in this chapter, put together your own Severity Spectrum by writing down three examples of misbehavior that your particular Little or Middle might engage in for each of the three levels of seventy (Minor Misbehavior, Standard Misbehavior, Serious Misbehavior).

Selecting the Right Spanking Implement For Your Little or Middle

For Caregivers, there are a great many potential Spanking Implements to be considered, each with their own unique advantages and disadvantages. To that end, this chapter will explore what qualities make up an effective Spanking Implement, and how to decide which Spanking Implement is the right one for your Little or Middle.

The Two Categories of Spanking Implement

All Spanking Implements can be placed into one of the following two categories: Short Range and Long Range. Short Range implements (your hand, hairbrushes, smaller paddles, etc.) tend to be the milder of the two variants due in large part to the fact that they have less length to build up momentum with while being swung through the air. (Although that isn't always the case as anyone who has ever been spanked with a particularly heavy hairbrush can tell you!) Whereas Long Range implements (belts, canes, switches, straps, etc.) tend to be more severe by nature of their greater lengths and striking range.

The type of implement you choose to use will determine the Spanking Positions available to you, so choose carefully!

The Two Types of Impact Sensation

Just as there are two categories of Spanking Implements, there are also two categories of Impact Sensations those Spanking Implements are capable of producing, namely: Sting, and Thud.

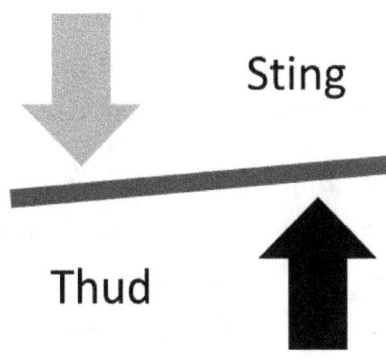

Stinging Implements

Just as the name would suggest, Stinging Implements create an intense but short-lived burning sensation confined to the surface of the area struck. Stinging Implements tend to be fairly light weight and flexible, with a broader striking surface that spreads the impact force of a swat out across a wide surface area rather than tightly focusing it to a single point. Therefore they are ideal for the sort of spanking where a burning bottom in the short term is the end goal, rather than prolonged discomfort sitting down after the fact.

Thudding Implements

Again, just as the name would suggest, Thudding Implements land with more "oomph" than their stinging counterparts. Thudding Implements are heavier than their stinging counterparts, and along with being more rigid, also tend to have a more compactly-focused striking surface. Rather than creating an intense but short-lived burning sensation, they instead strike deeper against a bottom or thighs to impart a long-lasting aching sensation that will remain with your Little or Middle long after their spanking is over.

Which Spanking Implement should I use?

While it is certainly tempting to think that there is no wrong answer to this question, the truth is that entirely depends on a few key factors.

- How severe of a spanking do you wish to give?
- What Spanking Positions are available to you at the moment?
- What Spanking Implements are available to you at the moment?
- Do you want the spanking you are about to give to leave behind a lingering ache that will make sitting down uncomfortable for your Little or Middle, or will a temporarily burning bottom be enough?

Moreover, very few Spanking Implements produce an entirely Stinging or Thudding Impact Sensation. Bearing this and the above questions in mind, the following chapter will provide you with a comprehensive list of recommended Spanking Implements, along with their relative strengths and weaknesses so that you as a

Caregiver can make an informed decision about what Spanking Implement will work best for your particular Little or Middle for any given spanking.

A Brief Note on the Importance of Implement Storage

As discussed earlier in Achieving Effective Discipline through Embarrassment, the effectiveness of a Little or Middle's spanking is determined long before the first swat is ever given, therefore it is paramount that your Little or Middle's Spanking Implements are not only easily accessible at a moment's notice, but also conspicuously visible as well.

Review What You've Learned

Complete the quiz below to test what you've learned so far. The correct answers can be found by turning the page over, so do your best and no cheating!

1. Which of the following are the two categories of Spanking Implement?

    a. Shot Range

    b. Long Range

    c. Both

2. The two types of Impact Sensations a Spanking Implement is capable of producing are _____.

    a. Mean and Bad

    b. Sting and Ouch

    c. Sting and Thud

    d. Smack and Whack

3. A Little or Middle's Spanking Implements should be kept out of sight until they are needed.

    a. True

    b. False

> Quiz Answers
> c. Both
> c. Sting and Thud
> b. False

Recommended Spanking Implements

While the potential number of implements a Caregiver could use to spank their Little or Middle are virtually infinite, the following are those that have been personally tested by this author and are guaranteed to achieve Effective Discipline.

The Hand

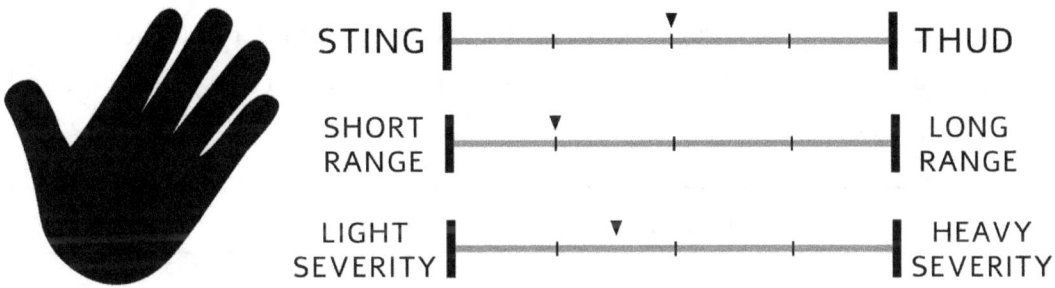

Academics in the field of Spankology have long debated whether or not the humble hand should count as a Spanking Implement or not, but it is this author's opinion that of course it should! Capable of producing both Stinging and Thudding Impact Sensations, The Hand is quite possibly the most versatile Spanking Implement available to a Caregiver.

Advantages as a Spanking Implement

- Can be used with any Spanking Position.
- Everyone has them and you always know where they are.
- A perfect middle ground between Sting and Thud.
- Capable of producing varying sensations with simple adjustments to your swatting technique.

Recommended Spanking Positions

- Over the Knee
- Bending Over
- Lying Facedown
- Diaper Position

Utilizing Proper Technique

Step 1. Remove any rings or bracelets you might be wearing and set them aside somewhere safe.

Step 2. If wearing long or restricting sleeves, roll them up so that they do not hamper your movements.

Step 3. While keeping your hand flat and rigid with your fingers together and your thumb out, raise your hand up to your shoulder and then send it back down again at speed, striking with the entirety of your palm and fingers.

Modulating Impact Sensation

With some minor changes to the way you hold your palm, you will be able to modulate the Impact Sensation your hand produces while spanking your Little or Middle.

Primarily Stinging Sensation

Keeping your fingers and thumb pressed firmly together and your hand in a loose cup, bring your palm down at speed as per usual while also snapping your wrist forward right before impact. Doing so will cause you to swat mostly with your fingertips and will sting far more than normal.

Primarily Thudding Sensation

Keeping your fingers and thumb splayed wide, angle your hand back, and strike entirely with the heel of your palm. Doing so will generate a Thudding Sensation that does not particularly sting.

The Wooden Spoon

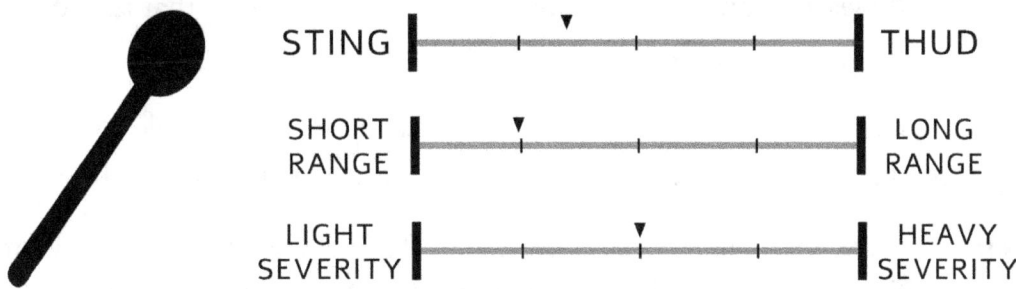

Found in just about any kitchen, The Wooden Spoon is an ideal Spanking Implement for any Caregiver wishing to give a spanking of any severity level.

Advantages as a Spanking Implement

- Can be used with any Spanking Position.
- Readily available and inexpensive to purchase.
- Its long handle and compact striking surface makes spanking specific spots of a Little or Middle's bottom and thighs a breeze, ensuring that you get an even, all-over red hue by the time their spanking is over every single time.
- Can be made extra severe simply by pre-soaking its head in warm water.

Recommended Storage Locations

This author recommends keeping a Wooden Spoon specifically dedicated for spanking your Little or Middle set aside either inside of a drawer in your kitchen, or else far enough back on top of your refrigerator where your Little or Middle will either have to stretch onto their tiptoes or retrieve a stepstool in order to reach it.

Recommended Spanking Positions

- Over the Knee
- Bending Over
- Lying Facedown
- Diaper Position

Utilizing Proper Technique

Step 1. If wearing long or restricting sleeves, roll them up so that they do not hamper your movements.

Step 2. Firmly grasp The Wooden Spoon by the base of its handle, making sure that its convex side is aimed toward the area you will be spanking.

Step 3. While maintaining a firm grip, bring The Wooden Spoon up to your shoulder and then back down again at speed, striking with only the convex side of its head.

The Hairbrush

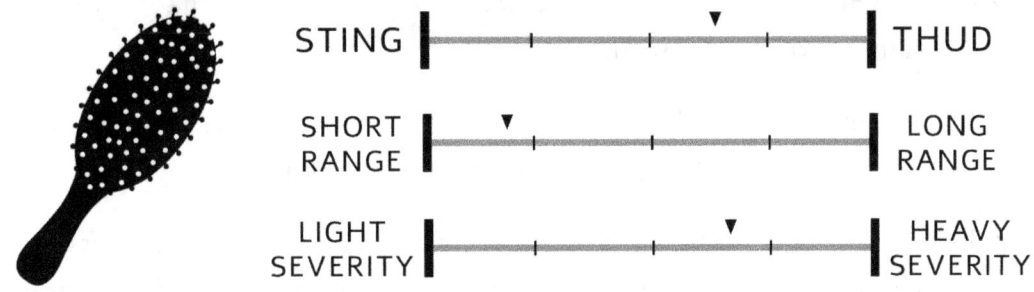

Readily available and conveniently portable, The Hairbrush is an excellent implement for any Caregiver wishing to give a moderate to severe spanking.

Advantages as a Spanking Implement

- Can be used with any Spanking Position.
- Readily available and inexpensive to purchase.
- Provides an excellent amount of Thudding Impact Sensation without sacrificing Sting.

Recommended Storage Locations

- This author recommends keeping a Hairbrush specifically dedicated for spanking your Little or Middle on top of their nightstand where it can serve as a silent reminder to behave themself when they go to bed, as well as when they wake up in the morning.
- If you as a Caregiver carry a purse or handbag, this author also recommends keeping another hairbrush inside of there for in case a spanking while out and about is necessary.

Recommended Spanking Positions

- Over the Knee
- Bending Over
- Lying Facedown
- Diaper Position

Utilizing Proper Technique

Step 1. If wearing long or restricting sleeves, roll them up so that they do not hamper your movements.

Step 2. Firmly grasp The Hairbrush by its handle, making sure that its bristles are facing away from where you will be spanking.

Step 3. While maintaining a firm grip, bring The Hairbrush up to your shoulder and then back down again at speed, striking with the smooth side of its head.

Choosing the Hairbrush That's Right for You

With so many different types of hairbrush available for purchase, picking the "right" one to use as a Spanking Implement can be a daunting task for any Caregiver. Worry not, though, dear reader, listed below are this author's personal recommendations, any of which (or all!) would make an excellent Spanking Implement.

Oval-Backed Brush

Typically made from denser materials and thus heavier, Oval-Backed Brushes produce a combination Stinging and Thudding Impact Sensation that truly is a force to be reckoned with for even the most obstinate of Littles and Middles by concentrating the impact force of each swat into a compact surface area of their bottom or thighs. As a result, they are ideal for any Caregiver wishing to give a spanking that will not only burn in the moment but leave their Little or Middle sitting uncomfortably long after their punishment is over.

Paddle Brush

With their broad backs and typically lightweight construction, the aptly named Paddle Brush distributes the impact force of each swat across a wide surface area of a Little or Middle's bottom or thighs, thus making them ideal for those Caregivers wishing to give a spanking that is primarily comprised of a Stinging Impact Sensation.

Vented Brush

Similar to Oval-Backed Brushes in their general shape, Vented Brushes are typically lighter and produce a far more pronounced Stinging Impact Sensation thanks to its enhanced aerodynamics stemming from the ventilation slits along its length.

Teasing Brush

Another aptly named option, Teasing Brushes are a slightly less severe alternative to their Oval-Backed counterparts, While a Teasing Brush also concentrates the impact force of a swat into a compact surface area of a Little or Middle's bottom or thighs, due to their lack of significant heft they impart more of a Stinging Impact Sensation with a minor lingering ache, thus making them ideal for those Caregivers wishing to give a swift Attitude Adjustment Spanking that will carry with it a little bit of lingering ache for their Little or Middle's bottom.

The Bath Brush

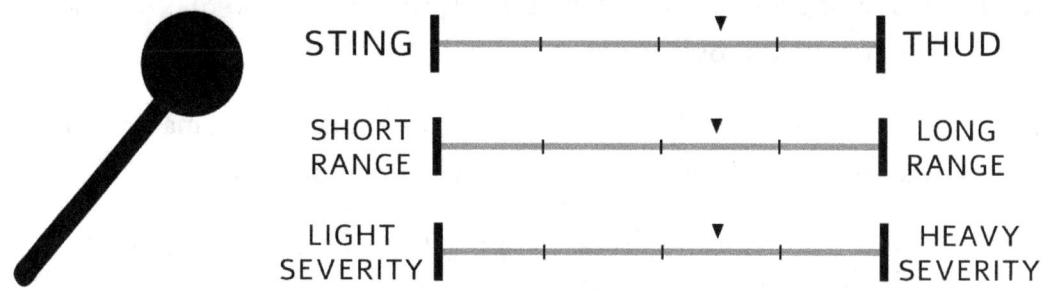

With its longer handle and broader head, The Bath Brush packs far more of a punch than its standard Hairbrush counterparts without the need for excess exertion on the part of the Caregiver, making it ideal for both moderate and severe spankings.

Advantages as a Spanking Implement

- Practical as both a bath time tool for scrubbing skin, as well as a Spanking Implement capable of imparting an exceptional amount of both Sting and Thud (especially on a wet bottom!) with every swat.
- Readily available and inexpensive to purchase. A sturdy, high-quality Bath Brush can typically be purchased from your local grocery store for as little as $4.

Recommended Storage Locations

This author recommends keeping a Bath Brush specifically dedicated for spanking your Little or Middle hanging up on a hook near the light switch of any bathroom your Little or Middle uses regularly.

Recommended Spanking Positions

- Bending Over
- Lying Facedown
- Diaper Position

Utilizing Proper Technique

Step 1. If wearing long or restricting sleeves, roll them up so that they do not hamper your movements.

Step 2. Firmly grasp The Bath Brush at the base of its handle, making sure that its bristles are facing away from where you will be spanking.

Step 3. While maintaining a firm grip, bring The Bath Brush up to your shoulder and then back down again at speed, making sure to pivot your hips with each impact in order to produce the maximum amount of follow-through possible.

The Paddle

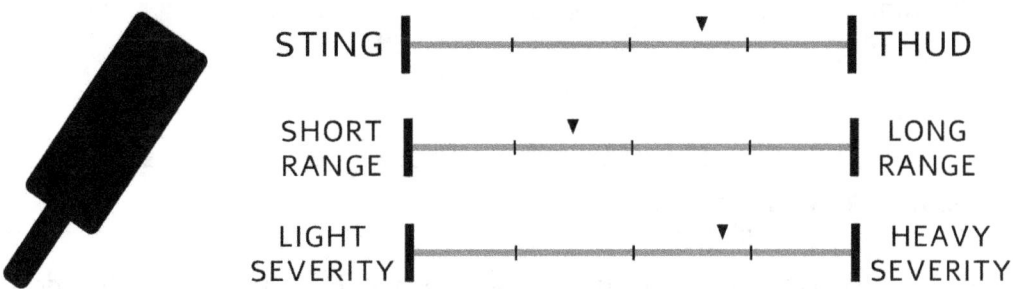

A tried and true implement of both the Midwest and south of the United States, The Paddle (sometimes referred to as The Board of Education) is an excellent choice for any Caregiver wishing to give a moderate to severe spanking that will leave their Little or Middle sitting uncomfortably long after it's over.

Advantages as a Spanking Implement

- Extremely sturdy. A well-made paddle will last you for many years to come.
- Provides an excellent amount of Thudding Impact Sensation without sacrificing Sting.
- Creating a personalized paddle for your Little or Middle is an excellent bonding exercise. Simply stop by your local big box craft store and pick up a pre-made sorority paddle (make sure it's a nice and durable one!) and some paint and glitter glue, and you're in for an evening of fun and sore bottoms!

Recommended Storage Locations

This author recommends keeping The Paddle hanging from a hook either by the back door to your home, or else beside the light switch in the bedroom of your Little or Middle. It is also highly recommended that you customize your Little or Middle's Paddle with either their name or a relevant (and of course embarrassing) phrase.

Recommended Spanking Positions

- Bending Over
- Lying Facedown
- Diaper Position

Utilizing Proper Technique

Step 1. If wearing long or restricting sleeves, roll them up so that they do not hamper your movements.

Step 2. Firmly grasp The Paddle by its handle.

Step 3. While maintaining a firm grip, bring The Paddle up to your shoulder and then back down again at speed against both bottom cheeks or thighs of your Little or Middle, making sure to pivot your hips with each impact so as to produce the maximum amount of follow-through possible.

The Slipper

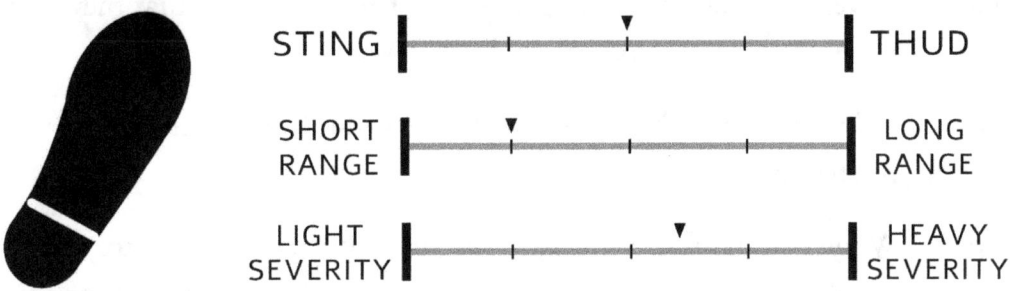

The Slipper (sometimes referred to as a Low Top Sneaker, Chankla, Plimsoll, or House Slipper) is a semi-flexible, rubber-soled shoe that provides an excellent balance between both Stinging and Thudding Impact Sensations for those Caregivers wishing to give a spanking that both burns in the moment and makes sitting down afterward a difficulty for any Little or Middle.

Advantages as a Spanking Implement

- Can be used with any Spanking Position.
- Readily available and inexpensive to purchase.
- Excellent balance of both Stinging and Thudding Impact Sensations.

Recommended Storage Locations

This author recommends keeping The Slipper on top of a coffee or end table in your home's living room, or else on top of the refrigerator in your home's kitchen.

Recommended Spanking Positions

- Over the Knee
- Bending Over
- Lying Facedown
- Diaper Position

Utilizing Proper Technique

Step 1. If wearing long or restricting sleeves, roll them up so that they do not hamper your movements.

Step 2. Grip The Slipper by its heel with its tread facing toward where you will be spanking.

Step 3. While maintaining a firm grip on The Slipper, bring it up to your shoulder and then back down again at speed, striking with the toe of The Slipper first for maximum impact force.

The Belt

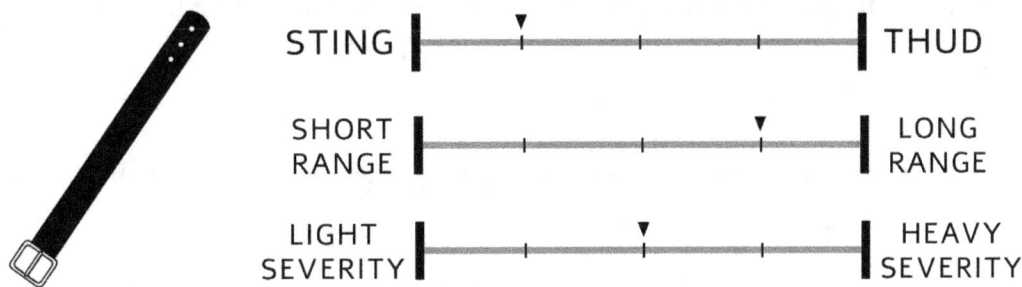

Another tried and true titan in the field of Spankology, The Belt provides an incredible amount of Stinging Impact Sensation thanks to the natural flexibility of leather, while also imparting just enough Thud to make sitting down after a spanking difficult for any Little or Middle.

Advantages as a Spanking Implement

- Affordable and easy to procure from any store with a clothing department.
- Perfect for those Caregivers who wear a belt day-to-day. You always have it with you!
- The phrase "Go get the belt" is guaranteed to have even the most obstinate of Littles and Middles immediately changing their behavior.

Recommended Storage Locations

If you do not plan on using The Belt you wear day-to-day as a Spanking Implement, this author recommends keeping The Belt on a hook on the inside of the door to your Little or Middle's closet where it can be seen every time they pick out clothes to wear for the day.

Recommended Spanking Positions

- Bending Over
- Lying Facedown
- Diaper Position

Utilizing Proper Technique

Step 1.   Remove The Belt from around your waist if you are currently wearing it, or else order your Little or Middle to bring it to you from wherever it is being stored.

Step 2.   If wearing long or restricting sleeves, roll them up so that they do not hamper your movements.

Step 3.   Fold The Belt in half and grip it just above where its buckle and tail end meet.

Step 4.   While maintaining a firm grip on The Belt, bring it up to your shoulder and then back down against both cheeks or thighs of your Little or Middle at speed, making sure to pivot your hips with each impact in order to produce the maximum amount of follow-through possible.

DON'T WORRY!

SOME CAREGIVERS FIND THEY HAVE A DIFFICULT TIME EQUALLY DISTRIBUTING THE IMPACT FORCE OF THE BELT AGAINST BOTH CHEEKS OR THIGHS OF THEIR LITTLE OR MIDDLE. IF YOU FIND YOURSELF EXPERIENCING THIS ISSUE, ADJUST YOUR AIM TO ONE CHEEK OR THIGH AT A TIME INSTEAD.

The Leather Strap

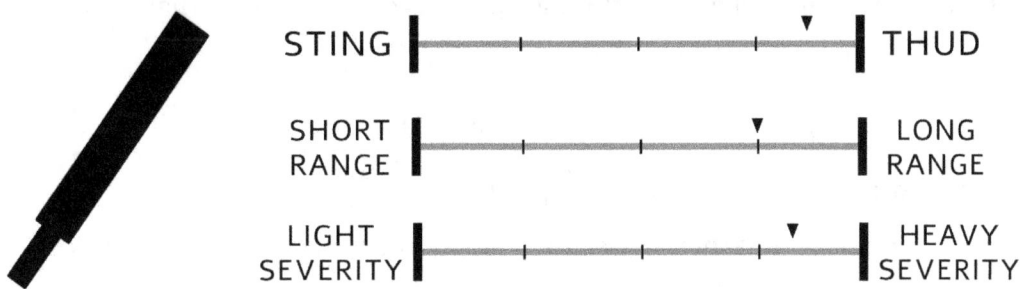

While at first glance it may seem very similar to The Belt, The Leather Strap is far more severe thanks to the added weight and rigidity of its denser construction, making it ideal for when a Caregiver intends on giving an extremely severe spanking that their Little or Middle won't soon forget.

Advantages as a Spanking Implement

- Extremely durable, and guaranteed to last decades with regular oiling.
- Dense enough to create burning welts and a long-lasting ache that will make sitting down after a spanking extremely uncomfortable for any Little or Middle, while still being flexible enough to conform to the shape of their bottom (and thighs) enough to not do any serious lasting damage when utilized correctly.

Recommended Storage Locations

This author recommends keeping The Leather Strap hanging from a hook either by the back door to your home, or else beside the light switch in the bedroom of your Little or Middle.

Recommended Spanking Positions

- Bending Over
- Lying Facedown
- Diaper Position

Utilizing Proper Technique

Step 1. If wearing long or restricting sleeves, roll them up so that they do not hamper your movements.

Step 2. Firmly grasp The Leather Strap at its base (or handle if it has one).

Step 3. While maintaining a firm grip, bring The Leather Strap up to your shoulder and then back down again at speed against both bottom cheeks or thighs of your Little or Middle, making sure to pivot your hips with each impact so as to produce the maximum amount of follow-through possible.

DON'T WORRY!

SOME CAREGIVERS FIND THEY HAVE A DIFFICULT TIME EQUALLY DISTRIBUTING THE IMPACT FORCE OF THE LEATHER STRAP AGAINST BOTH CHEEKS OR THIGHS OF THEIR LITTLE OR MIDDLE. IF YOU FIND YOURSELF EXPERIENCING THIS ISSUE, ADJUST YOUR AIM TO ONE CHEEK OR THIGH AT A TIME INSTEAD.

The Tawse

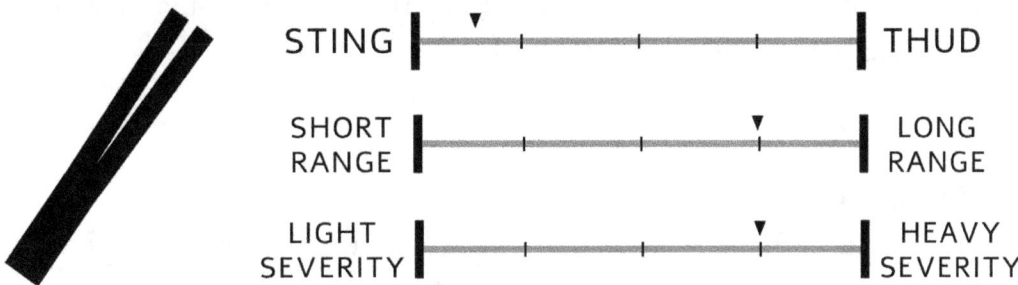

A Scottish twist on The Leather Strap, The Tawse favors imparting a severe Stinging Impact Sensation rather than the deeper Thudding Impact Sensation of its cousin The Leather Strap.

Advantages as a Spanking Implement

- Extremely durable, and guaranteed to last decades with regular oiling.
- Dense enough to create burning welts and a long-lasting ache that will make sitting down after a spanking extremely uncomfortable for any Little or Middle, while still being flexible enough to conform to the shape of their bottom (and thighs) enough to not do any serious lasting damage when utilized correctly.

Recommended Storage Locations

This author recommends keeping The Tawse hanging from a hook either by the back door to your home, or else beside the light switch in the bedroom of your Little or Middle.

Recommended Spanking Positions

- Bending Over
- Lying Facedown
- Diaper Position

Utilizing Proper Technique

Step 1. If wearing long or restricting sleeves, roll them up so that they do not hamper your movements.

Step 2. Firmly grasp The Tawse at its base (or handle if it has one).

Step 3. While maintaining a firm grip on The Tawse, bring it up to your shoulder and then back down again at speed against both bottom cheeks or thighs of your Little or Middle, making sure to pivot your hips with each impact so as to produce the maximum amount of follow-through possible.

DON'T WORRY!

SOME CAREGIVERS FIND THEY HAVE A DIFFICULT TIME EQUALLY DISTRIBUTING THE IMPACT FORCE OF THE TAWSE AGAINST BOTH CHEEKS OR THIGHS OF THEIR LITTLE OR MIDDLE. IF YOU FIND YOURSELF EXPERIENCING THIS ISSUE, ADJUST YOUR AIM TO ONE CHEEK OR THIGH AT A TIME INSTEAD.

The Cane

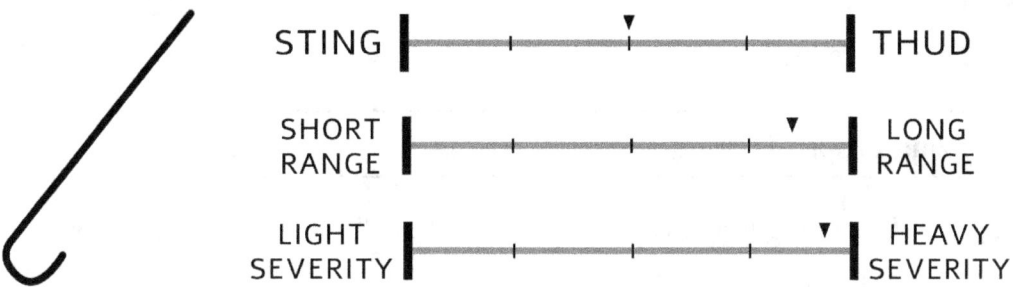

Six (or Twelve, or Eighteen, or even Twenty-Four!) of the Best is a proud tradition in the United Kingdom. As such, The Cane is a force to be reckoned with when it comes to dealing with those Littles and Middles who need a serious reminder to behave themselves.

Advantages as a Spanking Implement

- Its combination of weight and extreme flexibility makes it ideal for any Caregiver wishing to give a moderate to severe spanking.
- Severity can be modulated by adjusting the thickness of The Cane you as the Caregiver choose to use.
- The sound of a Cane whipping through the air can be enough on its own to get a Little or Middle to immediately change their behavior for the better, making it ideal for inspiring good behavior by making an example of a single Little or Middle.
- Leaves behind deep and vivid welts that that will make sitting comfortably an impossibility for even the most obstinate of Littles and Middles.

Recommended Storage Locations

This author recommends keeping The Cane hanging from a hook either by the back door to your home, or else beside the light switch in the bedroom of your Little or Middle.

Recommended Spanking Positions

- Bending Over
- Lying Facedown

Utilizing Proper Technique

Step 1. If wearing long or restricting sleeves, roll them up so that they do not hamper your movements.

Step 2. Firmly grasp The Cane at its base by its crook or handle.

Step 3. While maintaining a firm grip on The Cane, bring it up to your shoulder and then back down again at speed against both bottom cheeks or thighs of your Little or Middle, making sure to pivot your hips with each impact so as to produce the maximum amount of follow-through possible.

The Switch

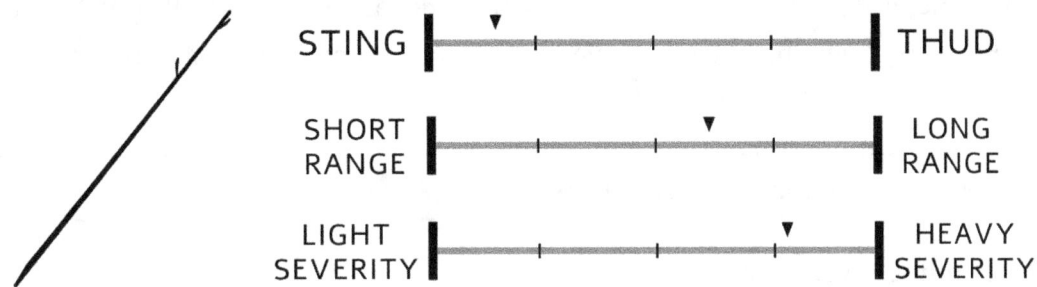

A proud tradition in the rural south of the United States, The Switch is not only an extremely effective Spanking Implement that is guaranteed to leave your Little or Middle sitting uncomfortably well after their spanking is over, but is also naturally biodegradable and eco-friendly!

Advantages as a Spanking Implement

- Abundant in nature and easily procured for free.
- Safe and effective to use on both the buttocks and thighs of your Little or Middle.
- Due to the preparation time required, the embarrassment of a Little or Middle can be greatly increased by baring their bottom prior to sending them out to cut a switch.
- The severity of the spanking you wish to give can be increased simply by having your Little or Middle cut and prepare multiple switches.
- The only Spanking Implement with a built-in timer. (All you have to do is keep swatting until it finally falls apart!)
- Leaves behind extremely vivid welts that, when paired with a particularly short pair of shorts or skirt, will ensure that your Little or Middle (along with any other Littles or Middles they happen to meet) will be on their very best behavior.

Recommended Storage Locations

If possible, it is highly recommended by this author to have a dedicated "Switching Bush" or "Switching Tree" in the yard of your home that your Little or Middle can be sent to in order to cut a switch.

Recommended Spanking Positions

- Bending Over
- Lying Facedown
- Diaper Position

Preparing a Switch the Correct Way

Unlike other Spanking Implements, a switch requires a mild amount of preparation before it can be put to use. Fortunately, the process is simple enough that even a Little or Middle can do it. (And should be required to!)

Step 1. Select a tree or bush with appropriate branches or growths that are green, thin, and flexible, such as those that can be found on a Crepe Myrtle or Hickory Tree.

Step 2. Using a pair of handheld pruning shears or a sharp pair of scissors, select at least one growth that is approximately as long as your arm from your elbow to the tips of your fingers, and cut it free.

Step 3. Using your hand, strip off any leaves growing from the switch.

Step 4. Using a pair of handheld pruning shears or a sharp pair of scissors, trim off any growths still protruding from the switch.

TIPS FOR TOPS!

DON'T WORRY IF YOU CAN'T GET YOUR SWITCH COMPLETELY SMOOTH. ANY LINGERING BUMPS OR UNEVENNESS HELP IT TO HURT THAT MUCH MORE.

Step 5. Finally, give your switch a few test swishes through the air to gauge its suitability for a spanking. It should produce an audible whipping sound as it cuts through the air.

TIPS FOR TOPS!

IF YOU'RE UNSURE WHETHER OR NOT THE SWITCH YOU'VE JUST PREPARED WILL GET THE JOB DONE, SIMPLY GIVE YOUR THIGH A COUPLE OF TEST SWATS. YOU'LL KNOW FOR CERTAIN THEN.

Utilizing Proper Technique

Step 1. Firmly grasp The Switch at its base with your dominant hand, and position yourself perpendicular to your Little or Middle.

Step 2. If wearing long or restricting sleeves, roll them up so that they do not hamper your movements.

Step 3. Maintaining a firm grip on the base of the switch with your dominant hand, repeatedly whip it down at as fast a pace as is comfortable for you as the Caregiver.

Note: Do not attempt to swing your switch "hard". Instead, let its natural speed and whippiness do the work for you.

Step 4. Continue applying the switch to the bottom and thighs of your Little or Middle until it has broken down to the point where it is no longer usable.

Step 5. Continue by repeating **Steps 3 and 4** for each additional switch your Little or Middle has prepared for their punishment.

Put It Into Action!

1) Using the information provided in this chapter, select three Spanking Implements that interest you and use at least one of them to give your Little or Middle a spanking this week.

2) Using the information provided in this chapter, select three potential Spanking Implements and then have your Little or Middle pick which one they would like to receive a Maintenance Spanking with.

REMEMBER!

SPANKING IS A TEAM SPORT, AND HONEST FEEDBACK FROM YOUR LITTLE OR MIDDLE IS PARAMOUNT TO ENSURING THAT THE SPANKINGS YOU GIVE THEM ARE AS EFFECTIVE AS POSSIBLE.

Selecting the Right Spanking Position for Your Little or Middle

There are several Spanking Positions a Caregiver has at their disposal, and understanding which to use with your particular Little or Middle is critical to giving a spanking that achieves Effective Discipline.

What to Consider When Choosing a Spanking Position

The size of the Little or Middle you intend to spank.

Some positions simply aren't feasible for bigger Littles and Middles, and that's just fine. Remember, the only thing that should be uncomfortable during a spanking is their bottom, so make sure the position you select is one that you both can be comfortable in for the entirety of their spanking.

The Spanking Implement you intend to use.

Long Range Spanking Implements require more room to swing than their short range counterparts, and as such make some Spanking Positions less practical than others. Fortunately for you, dear reader, all of the implements discussed in the chapter Recommended Spanking Implements all include a list of which Spanking Positions they work best with. So, when in doubt, double check the list!

What type of spanking do you intend to give?

Some Spanking Positions are naturally more embarrassing than others, making them potentially less appropriate for less severe spankings such as spankings for encouragement, emotional release, Maintenance Spankings, and Attitude Adjustment Spankings. However, as discussed in Achieving Effective Discipline through Embarrassment, Effective Discipline is built upon a foundation of embarrassment first and foremost, so don't feel like you must avoid the more embarrassing Spanking Positions just because the spanking you are about to give isn't going to be a particularly severe one.

Review What You've Learned

Complete the quiz below to test what you've learned so far. The correct answers can be found by turning the page over, so do your best and no cheating!

1. A Little or Middle's size should have no bearing on which Spanking Position a Caregiver chooses to use with them.

    a. True

    b. False

2. Long Range Spanking Implements can be used with any Spanking Position.

    a. True

    b. False

3. More embarrassing Spanking Positions should be avoided when giving a less severe spanking such as an Emotional Release Spanking or Attitude Adjustment Spanking.

    a. True

    b. False

Quiz Answers
b. False
b. False
b. False

Recommended Spanking Positions

While the number of potential positions a Caregiver could spank their Little or Middle in are virtually endless, the following are those that have been thoroughly tested by this author and are guaranteed to be both safe and effective for correcting your Little or Middle's misbehavior.

Over the Knee

Ideal for Short Range spanking implements, Over the Knee (Often abbreviated as OTK) is the tried and true Spanking Position. Devilishly simple, yet devastatingly effective, it's hard to go wrong with this position!

Advantages to the Over the Knee Position

- Ideal for longer spanking sessions.
- Comfortable for the Caregiver.
- Provides a small modicum of modesty for those Littles and Middles who hate having their private areas being put on display.
- Being draped facedown over a Caregiver's knee is an innately childish position, and as such is extra humbling for Middles.

Positioning Your Little or Middle

Step 1. Remove any keys, cellphones, or other objects from your front pockets and set them aside somewhere safe where you won't lose them.

Step 2. Find somewhere comfortable to sit. An armless chair is ideal, but any seat that does not have things blocking its sides will work just fine.

Step 3. Once settled, direct your Little or Middle to stand directly facing you, and then proceed to lower their pants or have them raise and hold their skirt or dress.

Step 4. If this is not an Attitude Adjustment Spanking, proceed to lower your Little or Middle's underwear, diaper, or pull-up as well.

Step 5. Conduct any pre-spanking scolding you might wish to give.

Step 6. Direct your Little or Middle to stand facing your thighs on the same side of your body as your dominant hand.

Step 7. Place your dominant hand along the small of your Little or Middle's back and gently but firmly guide them forward and down over your lap.

Step 8. Once in position, shift your Little or Middle forward until their bottom is centered atop your thighs. Ideally your Little or Middle's feet should no longer be touching the ground, but this is not required.

Step 9. Finally, place your non dominant hand along the small of your Little or Middle's back to help keep them in position, and proceed on with the rest of their spanking.

TIPS FOR TOPS!

FOR THOSE LITTLES OR MIDDLES WHO HAVE A TENDENCY TO BE EXTRA SQUIRMY DURING THEIR SPANKING, A CAREGIVER MAY WISH TO INSTEAD SHIFT THEIR GRIP TO THE SIDE OF THEIR LITTLE OR MIDDLE'S WAIST AND PULL THEM IN SNUGLY AGAINST THEIR FRONT TO KEEP THEM IN PLACE.

Compensating for Larger Littles and Middles

While spankings are obviously meant to be uncomfortable for your Little or Middle, that discomfort should be focused in their bottom or thighs. For those Littles and Middles who are too big to lay comfortably over their Caregiver's lap unsupported, simply swap out your armless chair for a couch, bed, bench, or any other seat where your Little or Middle's legs and torso can be supported.

Compensating for Uncooperative Littles and Middles

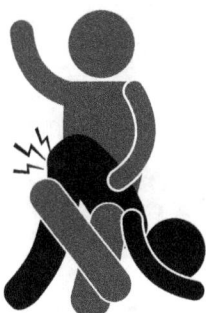

Even when a Little or Middle knows they deserve the spanking they are in the process of receiving, sometimes they just can't help but squirm and attempt to get off of your lap. In such cases, all you need do is shift the Little or Middle forward so that they are draped across the thigh on your non-dominant side, before then locking the leg on your dominant side over the backs of their knees, thereby pinning them into place.

Oh, and don't forget to throw in a few extra-hard swats for not cooperating!

Bending Over

Ideal for both Short Range and Long Range Spanking Implements, bending over is a tried and true Spanking Position that is perfect for when a shorter spanking is in order or a convenient place to sit down is not available.

Advantages to the Bending Over Position

- Perfect for shorter spankings and Attitude Adjustment Spankings
- Great for when you don't have a convenient place to sit down to give your Little or Middle a spanking.
- Allows a Caregiver to get a much wider swing, making it perfect for both Short Range and Long Range implements.

Positioning Your Little or Middle

Step 1. Select a location where you will be able to swing your dominant arm (and any Spanking Implement you choose to use) without hitting anything around you. (Watch out for overhead lights!)

Step 2. Lower your Little or Middle's pants, or have them raise up and hold their skirt or dress.

Step 3. If this is not an Attitude Adjustment Spanking, proceed to lower your Little or Middle's underwear, diaper, or pull-up as well.

Step 4. Conduct any pre-spanking scolding you might wish to give.

Step 5. Finally, direct your Little or Middle to bend over and place their hands on their knees.

Note: For those Caregivers wishing to give a more severe spanking, you may wish instead to direct your Little or Middle to grab their ankles (assuming they are flexible enough to do so without major risk of falling over). Doing so will pull the skin and muscles over their bottom more taut, ensuring there is less padding to absorb individual swats, leading to an overall more painful spanking.

Helpful Variations

Sometimes, having your Little or Middle bend over and grab their knees (or ankles) just isn't an option. Whether it's because they have an issue maintaining their balance, holding still for the duration of their spanking, or you yourself as the Caregiver wish for them to be positioned in a more stable way for a prolonged spanking, the Bending Over Spanking Position can easily be modified to meet your needs. Simply have your Little or Middle either lean up against a wall and push their bottom out, or else bend them over the back of a high-backed chair or couch (great for when they're misbehaving in the living room), the side of a sturdy table (great for a spanking during dinnertime), or a bed (great for a spanking right before bedtime).

Yes, it really is that easy!

Lying Facedown

Ideal in particular for Long Range Spanking Implements, positioning your Little or Middle facedown atop a bed or couch is perfect for the Caregiver wishing to give a more severe or prolonged spanking.

Advantages to the Lying Facedown Position

- Perfect for longer or more severe spankings.
- Allows a Caregiver to get as wide a swing as possible.
- The most comfortable position (relatively speaking) for a Little or Middle to be spanked in since their entire body is being supported.
- Great for if you plan on putting your Little or Middle into a diaper or pull-up after their spanking. Just roll them over once you're done!

Positioning Your Little or Middle

Step 1. Select a location such as a bed or couch where your Little or Middle will be able to comfortably lie facedown, and you will be able to swing your dominant arm (and any Spanking Implement you might choose to use) without hitting yourself or anything around you. (Watch out for overhead lights!)

Step 2. Pile up at least two pillows in the middle of the bed or couch where your Little or Middle's hips will rest. Doing this elevates their bottom and sit-spots, positioning them exactly where they should be for their spanking.

Step 3. Lower your Little or Middle's pants, or have them raise up and hold their skirt or dress.

Step 4. If this is not an Attitude Adjustment Spanking, proceed to lower your Little or Middle's underwear, diaper, or pull-up as well.

Step 5. Conduct any pre-spanking scolding you might wish to give.

Step 6. Finally, direct your Little or Middle to lie facedown atop the bed or couch you have selected for their spanking, making sure that their hips are positioned directly over the pillows you piled up in **Step 2**.

Increasing Severity with a Raised Bottom

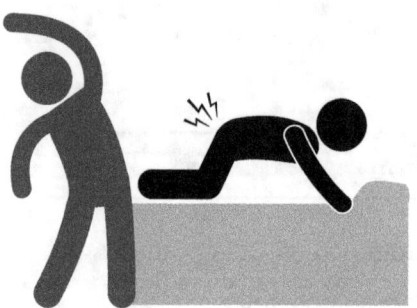 

In cases where a particularly severe spanking is required, simply adjust the position of your Little or Middle's hips so that their bottom is elevated up high and their head and shoulders are pressed down into the bed or couch they are lying on. Not only will doing so pull the skin of their bottom or thighs taut, thereby greatly increasing the amount of Impact Force for each swat by reducing those area's natural shock absorption capabilities, but also causes your Little or Middle's bottom cheeks naturally part to expose their anus and genitalia as well increasing their embarrassment.

This secondary effect in particular is extremely useful for the Caregiver wishing to follow up their Little or Middle's spanking with a Supplementary Punishment such as figging or an enema.

The Diaper Position

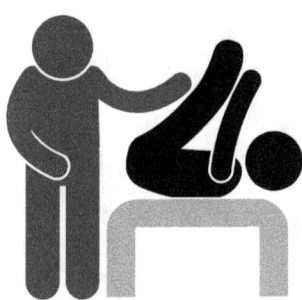

Ideal in particular for Short Range spanking implements, the Diaper Position is at once both extremely embarrassing (especially for Middles) and one of the most uncomfortable positions to be spanked in.

Advantages to the Diaper Position

- By its very nature, the Diaper Position is an extremely childish position to be placed in, especially for Middles. As a result, it sends a very clear message to your Little or Middle, namely: "If you want to act like a child, then I will treat you like one."
- Increases the amount of Impact Force per individual swat by keeping the bottom and thighs of your Little or Middle pulled taut, thereby greatly reducing their natural shock absorption capabilities.
- Leaves the genitals and anus of your Little or Middle completely exposed, thereby greatly increasing their overall embarrassment.
- Perfect for those Caregivers wishing to follow up a spanking by putting their Little or Middle into a diaper or pull-up. After all, they're already in position!

Positioning Your Little or Middle

Step 1. Select a stable platform for your Little or Middle to lie down on, such as a bed, couch, kitchen table, or diaper changing station in a public restroom.

Step 2. Lower your Little or Middle's pants and help them to step out of them. If your Little or Middle is wearing a dress or skirt, have them take it off entirely so as to not have it become wrinkled.

Step 3. If this is not an Attitude Adjustment Spanking, proceed to lower your Little or Middle's underwear, diaper, or pull-up and help them step out of it.

Step 4. Neatly fold and set aside your Little or Middle's now discarded clothing. This will give them ample opportunity to reflect on their actions and what is about to happen, increase their overall embarrassment, and ensure that their clothing does not become wrinkled.

Step 5. Conduct any pre-spanking scolding you might wish to give.

Step 6. Help your Little or Middle up onto the platform you chose in **Step 1**.

Step 7. Direct your Little or Middle to lie down on their back.

Step 8. Finally, take hold of your Little or Middle by their ankles and lift their legs up until their hips begin to rise up off of the platform they are lying on.

TIPS FOR TOPS!

DEPENDING ON THE SIZE OF YOUR LITTLE OR MIDDLE, IT MAY BE MORE COMFORTABLE FOR BOTH THEM AND YOU TO HAVE THEM WRAP THEIR ARMS AROUND THEIR KNEES TO HELP KEEP THEIR LEGS IN POSITION ONCE THEY'VE BEEN RAISED UP.

Giving a Spanking the Correct Way

In this chapter we will explore in-depth the process by which a Caregiver should give a spanking, be it for punishment, encouragement, maintenance, or emotional release.

When Should a Spanking Take Place?

Requiring your Little or Middle to wait for a spanking after they have earned one will cause them undue mental and emotional stress as the prospect of their upcoming punishment looms over them. Moreover, delaying a spanking also introduces the potential for a Little or Middle to entertain the notion that perhaps their Caregiver will forget to spank them if they can simply stall long enough while behaving themself. Which, while on the surface may sound like a positive outcome since it would mean your Little or Middle is behaving themself, their motivation for doing so is nevertheless rooted in attempting to avoid earned consequences rather than because they know it is the right thing to do, which is entirely antithetical to the philosophy of Effective Discipline. Therefore, a spanking should always be given as soon as possible.

REMEMBER!

SWIFT DISCIPLINE IS EFFECTIVE DISCIPLINE, SO DON'T DELAY A SPANKING WHEN ONE IS DUE!

Where Should a Spanking Take Place?

Given the necessity for a spanking to be given as soon as possible after it has been earned, the natural next question a Caregiver might ask themself is just where said spanking should take place? Again, the answer to this question (like many things when it comes to giving a spanking the correct way) is quite simple. When possible, a Caregiver should spank their Little or Middle at the scene of their misbehavior, be that over your knee at the kitchen table during dinner, in the diaper position on top of a changing table in a family restroom while grocery shopping, or bending over a park bench while out at the playground.

Granted, circumstances do not always make this possible. For instance, a Caregiver cannot honestly be expected to spank their Little or Middle in the middle of a crowded movie theater for talking too much during a showing, now can they? In cases such as these, a Caregiver should instead endeavor to spank their Little or Middle somewhere close by that is both safe for their Little or Middle and where their punishment will be unlikely to be interrupted. (Family restrooms are always an excellent option.)

A Brief Note Regarding Witnesses to a Spanking

As discussed earlier in *Achieving Effective Discipline through Embarrassment*, Effective Discipline starts long before the first swat of a spanking is ever given. To that end, a Caregiver should not shy away from spanking their Little or Middle just because someone else is there to see them reap the rewards of their misbehavior. On the contrary, not only will having others witness their punishment help to make it both more effective in the short term and memorable in the long run for your Little or Middle, but doing so will also serve as a valuable community service by demonstrating in no uncertain terms to any Littles and Middles around you exactly what they can expect should they choose to misbehave as well.

A Proper Spanking is a Spanking on the Bare Bottom, Always!

It is tempting for some Caregivers to assume that a spanking given on a Little or Middle's underwear or panties is virtually identical to a spanking given on their bare bottom, but that could not be further from the truth! In fact, spanking Littles and Middles on their bare bottom is critical to ensuring that every spanking they receive achieves Effective Discipline, and outlined below are the key reasons why.

A Little or Middle's underwear or panties are capable of absorbing up to 20% of an individual swat's Impact Force.

You wouldn't accept your Little or Middle only behaving themself 80% of the time, would you? Of course you wouldn't! So then, why would you accept giving a spanking that is only 80% effective?

A spanking on a bare bottom helps to create the necessary headspace for Effective Discipline to be achieved.

Not only is having your naked bottom exposed for all to see extremely embarrassing for any Little or Middle (especially for Middles), but doing so also helps to facilitate the necessary headspace your Little or Middle will need to occupy in order for their spanking to be both effective in the short term and memorable in the long run, thereby ensuring that they will behave themself in the future.

A bare bottom ensures that a Caregiver has all the information they need to make a spanking as effective as possible.

When a Little or Middle's bottom is fully bared, a Caregiver is able to see exactly how effective their individual swats are by gauging the gradual shifts in skin color as areas begin to redden and can therefore modulate their speed and force as needed. Moreover, a bare bottom also enables a Caregiver to see what areas of their Little or Middle's bottom and thighs may need more (or less) attention, thereby ensuring that the end result of their spanking is a thoroughly punished (as well as equally punished) bottom and thighs.

Preparing Your Little or Middle for Their Spanking

As has been stated repeatedly throughout this book, Effective Discipline starts long before the first swat of a spanking is ever given. To that end, the way in which a Caregiver goes about preparing their Little or Middle to receive said first swat is paramount. Thankfully, the actual mechanics of preparing a Little or Middle for their spanking are remarkably straightforward, and so long as a Caregiver adheres to the steps outlined below, they will be guaranteed to give their Little or Middle the Effective Discipline they so dearly need whenever it comes time for their bottom to be bared for a spanking.

Step 1. *(Optional)* Place your Little or Middle into the corner for a pre-spanking time out, making sure to follow the steps outlined in the *Utilizing Corner Time the Correct Way* subsection of the *Recommended Supplementary Punishments* chapter.

Step 2. Calmly explain to your Little or Middle exactly what they did that was wrong and why it was wrong, along with how they can behave better in the future. Make sure you avoid any "You are" statements that would imply your Little or Middle is intrinsically bad.

Incorrect: "Rhen, I can't believe you didn't do your homework, you bad girl!"

Correct: "Rhen, I am disappointed that you chose not to do your homework when you got home. Next time you need to do it before you play video games, am I understood?"

Step 3.   Calmly explain to your Little or Middle that because of what you discussed in **Step 2,** you are now going to give them a spanking. Make sure to emphasize that even though you are going to have to punish them, that you still love them, and that they are still a good boy, girl, or non-binary sweetheart who just made a mistake.

Incorrect: "Get over my lap, you little brat! You're getting a spanking."

Correct: "Because you chose to do something you know was naughty, I'm going to spank you now. Once we're done with that, though, you'll be my good girl again, won't you, honey?"

Step 4.   If you plan on using a Spanking Implement and do not have it on hand already, instruct your Little or Middle to go collect it and bring it to you.

Step 5.   Bare your Little or Middle's bottom and position them by following the "Utilizing Proper Technique" instructions for whichever Spanking Position you have decided to use for this particular punishment.

Step 6.   At this point, if you so desire, deliver any last minute lecturing you might feel is justified. With your Little or Middle in position with their bare bottom exposed, you are guaranteed their complete and undivided attention, so make sure you take full advantage of it!

Increasing Severity with Water, Baby Oil, and Capsaicin Cream

When an extra dose of severity is called for during a spanking, a Caregiver can achieve excellent results by the simple addition of rubbing any of the following materials into the bottom and thighs of their Little or Middle prior to giving them their spanking.

Water

Keeping a Little or Middle's bottom and thighs wet with water during the course of their spanking helps to make each individual swat sting a great deal more, and also leads to (rather lovely in this author's opinion) bruising. Making it an ideal augmentation for those Caregivers wishing to give a spanking that will be at the forefront of their Little or Middle's mind long after the act itself is over.

Baby Oil

Similar in many regards to spanking on a wet bottom using water, rubbing in a healthy dose of baby oil (or comparable lotion) into a Little or Middle's bottom and thighs prior to their spanking will radically increase the amount of sting each individual swat imparts.

Capsaicin Cream

Capsaicin is the compound inside of chili peppers that makes your mouth burn, and when applied in lotion form to your Little or Middle's bottom and thighs prior to a spanking, it will have them burning just as much even before the swats start falling!

WARNING!

MAKE SURE NOT TO GET ANY CAPSAICIN CREAM IN THE EYES, MOUTH, OR GENITALS OF YOURSELF OR YOUR LITTLE OR MIDDLE. THE LATTER IN PARTICULAR IS NO FUN AT ALL, TRUST ME.

Where to Aim During a Spanking

The chart below highlights the areas a Caregiver should focus their efforts on (as well as avoid) during a spanking.

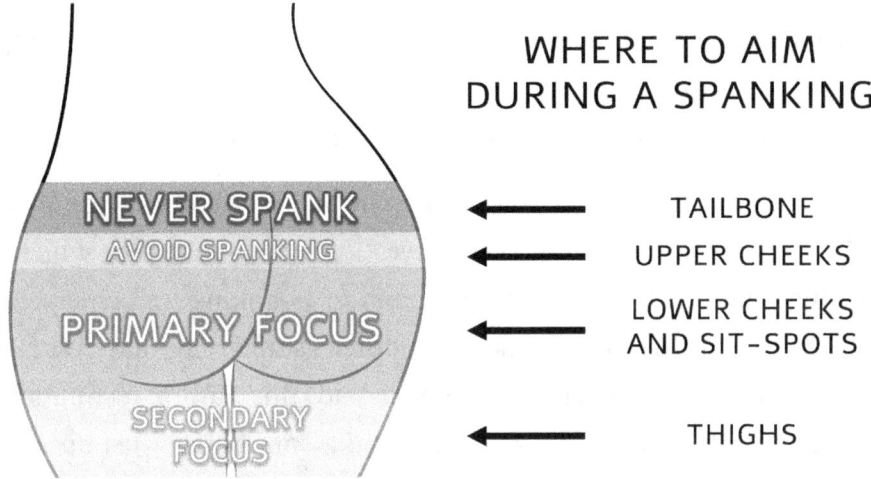

As you can see, the individual swats of a Little or Middle's spanking should primarily be focused along the lower half of their bottom cheeks, paying particular attention to the crease where their bottom and thighs meet (aka. their sit-spots, because that is where their weight primarily rests while sitting).

However, a Caregiver should also not neglect the thighs of their Little or Middle either! Naturally less padded compared to their bottom cheek counterparts, the thighs are an excellent area to swat when you need to drive a particular point home while spanking your Little or Middle, or when you wish to create lingering soreness that will stick with your Little or Middle after their spanking is over.

Augmenting Severity by Targeting Inner Thighs and the Anus

While the backs of a Little or Middle's thighs are already extra sensitive when compared to their bottom cheeks, their inner thighs are significantly worse. Therefore, when the need for a more severe spanking arises, a Caregiver need only push their Little or Middle's legs apart and swat along the inside of their thighs.

Alternatively, a Caregiver can spread their Little or Middle's bottom cheeks apart using the fingers of their non-dominant hand to expose their anus, before then focusing their swatting directly atop it. Not only is this area even more sensitive than a Little or Middle's inner thighs, spanking their anus has the additional benefit of being extremely embarrassing (especially for Middles). Moreover, this technique also synergizes particularly well with Supplementary Punishments such as figging and enemas.

Crafting the Perfect Swat

Speed vs. Power

The speed with which a spanking is given should be approximately one to two swats per second, adjusting as necessary for the weight of the Spanking Implement being used, along with a Caregiver's personal comfort levels. Remember, you're punishing your Little or Middle's bottom and thighs, not your rotator cuff!

As for the amount of power that should be put behind each individual swat of a spanking, there is unfortunately no objective "kiloswat" metric by which a Caregiver can gauge the Impact Force of their hand or Spanking Implement. Just how hard you choose to spank your Little or Middle is something that you as a Caregiver must gauge in the moment. That being said, this author recommends conserving one's strength and aiming for achieving a sore bottom via an abundance of relatively painful swats, as opposed to a few extremely hard ones.

Don't Forget the Follow-Through!

All of the speed and power in the world cannot make up for a swat that is delivered without proper follow-through. Remember, you are spanking your Little or Middle, not the topmost layer of skin of their bottom and thighs. Therefore, when you deliver a swat, make sure that swat is delivered with full follow-through by not stopping short right at impact.

How Long Should a Spanking Be?

Again, just as there is no objective "kiloswat" metric by which a Caregiver can gauge how hard they should spank their Little or Middle, there is likewise no strict rule on exactly how long a spanking should take place for.

That being said, this author is a firm believer that spanking for results, rather than a particular number of swats, is the best way to achieve Effective Discipline. To that end, it is recommended that a Caregiver spank their Little or Middle for at minimum five minutes, before then continuing on in one-minute intervals until the desired amount of contrition (be that tears, promises to be good, apologies, etc.) and overall redness have both been achieved.

REMEMBER!

SPANKING IS A TEAM SPORT! MAKE SURE YOU LISTEN TO WHAT YOUR LITTLE OR MIDDLE IS TELLING YOU IN THE MOMENT AS YOU PUNISH THEM. YOU'LL KNOW WHEN THEY'VE LEARNED THEIR LESSON. AND, IF FOR SOME REASON YOU END UP NOT SPANKING THEM FOR AS LONG AS MAYBE YOU SHOULD HAVE, DON'T WORRY, THERE'S ALWAYS NEXT TIME.

Finishing a Spanking the Correct Way

Bringing a spanking to a close is a relatively simple process, however there are certain steps that must be followed in order for the spanking that has just been given to achieve Effective Discipline and not just a sore bottom.

Step 1. While keeping your Little or Middle in position, gently rub their bottom and murmur soothing words as you allow them the time they need to calm their breathing.

   Example: "There there, sweetheart, it's over now. I'm proud of you, you took that spanking so well."

Step 2. Ease your Little or Middle back onto their feet and give them a hug and kiss and reinforce how proud you are of them for taking their punishment like a big girl, boy, or non-binary sweetheart.

Step 3. (Optional) Place your Little or Middle into the corner for a ten minute time out, making sure to follow the steps outlined in the *Utilizing Corner Time the Correct Way* subsection of the *Recommended Supplementary Punishments* chapter. This is an excellent option for those Littles or Middles who need additional time to rein themselves in, as well as for those Littles or Middles who need additional time to contemplate their misbehavior and how they will act differently in the future.

Step 4. (Optional) If this was a Spanking for emotional release or an Encouragement Spanking, you may wish to rub lotion or arnica gel into the bottom and thighs of your Little or Middle to ease their sting and help them to further relax.

Step 5. Proceed with giving your Little or Middle any additional Supplementary Punishments they still have coming.

Step 6. (Optional) Make an entry in your Little or Middle's official Spanking Diary (sold separately) for this particular punishment.

Dealing With Uncooperative Littles and Middles

While, in theory, your Little or Middle should be well-behaved enough to fully cooperate with their punishment when a spanking has been earned, sometimes flights of disobedience get the better of them. When such circumstances arise, worry not! Simply follow the steps outlined below and you will have your Little or Middle back on track in no time.

Step 1. Take hold of your Little or Middle by their shoulders and look them directly in the eye.

Step 2. Ask them if the way they are currently behaving is how they know they should be.

Step 3. Explain to them in no uncertain terms that they will be getting spanked, whether they like it or not, and that they can either cooperate now, or else go into the corner until they are ready to do so.

Step 4. If your Little or Middle continues to be uncooperative at this point, place them into the corner for a ten minute time out, making sure to follow the steps outlined in the *Utilizing Corner Time the Correct Way* subsection of the *Recommended Supplementary Punishments* chapter.

Step 5. After their time out is over, continue with the punishment your Little or Middle has earned.

Step 6. (Optional) Inform your Little or Middle that they have earned an additional spanking before bedtime that evening for not cooperating with their punishment.

> ### Review What You've Learned

Complete the quiz below to test what you've learned so far. The correct answers can be found by turning the page over, so do your best and no cheating!

1. There is no rush to get to a spanking after one has been earned.

    a. True

    b. False

2. A Caregiver should avoid spanking their Little or Middle where others can watch.

    a. True

    b. False

3. There is no wrong place to spank a Little or Middle's bottom.

    a. True

    b. False

4. Spankings should be limited to a specific number of swats.

    a. True

    b. False

5. A Little or Middle should be sent away immediately after their spanking is over.

    a. True

    b. False

> **Quiz Answers**
> b. False
> b. False
> b. False
> b. False
> b. False

Put It Into Action!

1) Using the information in this chapter, give your Little or Middle a Disciplinary Spanking the correct way this week.

2) After spanking your Little or Middle, write down what parts of the process were the easiest for you and what parts you felt you struggled with. Then, write down three ways you feel you could improve for the next time you spank your Little or Middle.

Utilizing Behavior Contracts to Achieve Effective Discipline

Providing your Little or Middle with a clear roadmap to good behavior is critical to achieving Effective Discipline. After all, no Caregiver should ever punish their Little or Middle for acting in ignorance. To that end, it is this author's recommendation that Caregivers establish a list of rules and expectations for their Little or Middle to adhere to in the form of a Behavior Contract.

Behavior Contracts are a Team Effort

Unlike with a spanking where a Little or Middle need not initially be in agreement that they need to be punished in order for Effective Discipline to be achieved, a Behavior Contract is something that both a Caregiver and their Little or Middle must be in complete agreement with in order for it to be truly effective. Therefore, rather than being a list of rules and dictates handed down from on high, a Behavior Contract should instead be something that you and your Little or Middle create together. So, sit down with your Little or Middle, welcome their input, and strive to create a series of rules and expectations that you both can be happy with.

Remember to Keep it Simple, Silly!

Rather than being a multipage tome of granular regulations, complex point systems, and branching if/then statements, the content of a Behavior Contract should be clear and concise. For example, rather than creating a list of every possible bad word your Little or Middle is forbidden from saying, instead make it a rule that your Little or Middle must always speak with respect. Doing so not only covers all potential profanity, but also carries the added benefit of nipping any potential backtalk in the bud as well!

An Effective Contract is a Visible Contract

A Behavior Contract is only as useful as it is easy to refer to, and neither you nor your Little or Middle should be expected to have it memorized. To that end, it is this author's recommendation that you make two laminated copies of the Behavior Contract you and your Little or Middle put together, keeping one pinned to your refrigerator with a magnet, and the other taped to the front of their bedroom door. Doing so will ensure that you and your Little or Middle always have your Behavior Contract on hand and ready to refer to whenever the need may arise.

The Four Components of an Effective Behavior Contract

A Behavior Contract that is conducive to achieving Effective Discipline is one that is comprised of the following four items.

The Responsibilities of the Little or Middle

This section should contain a series of bullet points enumerating the specific standards of behavior you as the Caregiver expect your Little or Middle to adhere to.

A Clear and Concise List of House Rules

This section should consist of bullet points enumerating the specific rules for the home you and your Little or Middle share together.

A Section Outlining Potential Rewards for Good Behavior

Some Caregivers may be tempted to argue that good behavior is its own reward, but it has long been established in the field of Spankology that positive reinforcement is equally as important as swift consequences for misbehavior when it comes to fostering an environment where Effective Discipline can be achieved. To that end, you and your Little or Middle should choose at least three potential rewards for good behavior to be included in the Behavior Contract you create together.

A Signature Block

A Behavior Contract should end with a statement acknowledging that your Little or Middle agrees to adhere to rules and expectations outlined above and that they understand they will be spanked should they misbehave, followed by a place for you, the Caregiver, and them to both sign, making it nice and official.

Example Behavior Contract

The following Behavior Contract can be used as a blueprint for creating your own Behavior Contract with your Little or Middle!

Rhen promises to:

- Be honest and respectful when she speaks.
- Make sure her room is neat and tidy at all times.
- Achieve at least a 94% on all of her assignments.
- Finish all of her homework as soon as she gets home from class for the day.
- Drink at least three glasses of water every day.
- Obey all house rules.

Our House Rules are:

- No shoes past the entryway.
- No slamming doors.
- Bedtime is at 10:30 on school nights, and 11:30 on non-school nights.
- After eating, rinse off your dishes and put them in the dishwasher.
- Only one can (or bottle!) of soda per day.

When Rhen behaves herself, Dana promises to:

- Let Rhen pick where we eat once a week.
- Buy Rhen a new video game every month.
- Buy Rhen a new book every two weeks.
- Let Rhen have an extra soda before bedtime on Fridays.
- Extend Rhen's bedtime by an extra hour on the weekend.

I understand the rules above and I promise to obey. I understand that when I behave well I will receive a reward, but I also agree that if I misbehave I will be spanked as a punishment.

Dana Johnson
Caregiver's Signature

Rhen Mathews
Little / Middle's Signature

Review What You've Learned

Complete the quiz below to test what you've learned so far. The correct answers can be found by turning the page over, so do your best and no cheating!

1. A Little or Middle's input is not required when creating a Behavior Contract.

    a. True

    b. False

2. Behavior Contracts should be kept somewhere visible at all times.

    a. True

    b. False

3. A Behavior Contract should include a section for potential rewards for good behavior.

    a. True

    b. False

Quiz Answers
b. False
a. True
a. True

Put It Into Action!

Using the information in this chapter, sit down with your Little or Middle this week and create your own Behavior Contract.

Achieving Effective Discipline via Delegation of Spanking Authority

Just as it takes a village to raise a child, so too should the discipline of your Little or Middle not be constrained to just yourself as their Primary Caregiver. Spanking is a team sport, after all, and as such, it requires a team! Teachers, Babysitters, "Aunts", "Uncles", and sometimes even older "siblings" should all be active participants in ensuring that your Little or Middle is on their best behavior at all times, even when you're not there to keep an eye on them.

REMEMBER!

CONSISTENCY IS KEY WHEN IT COMES TO ACHIEVING EFFECTIVE DISCIPLINE!

To that end, it is this author's fervent recommendation that you reach out to those involved in a Caregiving capacity in the life of your Little or Middle and invite them to help you mind your charge via what is known in Spankology as a Spanking Permission Form.

What is a Spanking Permission Form?

A Spanking Permission Form is a micro-contract between you, the Primary Caregiver, and a trusted third-party Secondary Caregiver you wish to grant disciplinary rights over your Little or Middle. In brief, it should consist of a written request for the Secondary Caregiver to assist you in helping your Little or Middle to maintain good behavior through the judicious application of Effective Discipline when necessary.

Now, while this may sound like a terribly dense set of forms and legalese, allow me to assure you that it is anything but. In fact, below is an example of a perfectly-executed Spanking Permission Form which should serve as a template for your own Little or Middle's Spanking Permission Forms.

> I hereby grant the Secondary Caregiver signed below permission to discipline my Little or Middle (signed below) as they see fit should they misbehave while I am not present in order to help them maintain good behavior at all times.
>
> Signed,
>
> *Dana Johnson*
> Primary Caregiver
>
> *Alana Pierson*
> Secondary Caregiver
>
> *Rhen Mathews*
> Little / Middle

See? It really is that easy!

How much disciplinary authority should a Secondary Caregiver be granted?

Whether or not a Spanking Permission Form should grant a Secondary Caregiver carte blanche to punish your Little or Middle as they see fit, or else limit them to a specific set of disciplinary options is entirely up to you as your Little or Middle's Primary Caregiver. For some Secondary Caregivers, such as Babysitters or older "siblings", it may be wise to limit their disciplinary toolset to just spanking as they may not be fully qualified to give your Little or Middle anything more severe, whereas someone more experienced such as a Teacher, "Aunt", or "Uncle" would be someone you could trust with free reign regarding the discipline of your Little or Middle. In the end, though, the choice is entirely up to you and you should go with whatever you feel comfortable with.

A note regarding less-experienced Secondary Caregivers

It is this author's recommendation that if you harbor any reservations regarding a potential Secondary Caregiver's ability to discipline your Little or Middle effectively, that you should gift them a copy of this book and invite them to read it. That way, you can both rest assured that you are on the same page regarding how Effective Discipline should be achieved with your Little or Middle.

Review What You've Learned

Complete the quiz below to test what you've learned so far. The correct answers can be found by turning the page over, so do your best and no cheating!

1. A Spanking Permission Form needs to be multiple pages of complicated legalese.

    a. True

    b. False

2. Only very experienced disciplinarians should be considered as potential Secondary Caregivers for your Little or Middle.

    a. True

    b. False

3. How many people should be offered Spanking Permission Forms for your Little or Middle?

    a. 1 Person

    b. 2 People

    c. 5 People

    d. As many people as possible!

Quiz Answers
b. False
b. False
d. As many people as possible!

Put It Into Action!

1) This week, sit down with your Little or Middle and prepare Spanking Permission Forms for at least three potential Secondary Caregivers.

2) Together with your Little or Middle, deliver the Spanking Permission Forms you prepared to each Secondary Caregiver you chose in the previous assignment item.

Congratulations!

If you've made it this far, then congratulations! You are now legally qualified as a Novice Spankologist. On the following page you will find a Certificate of Completion just for you. Simply sign your name where indicated, and you will have officially graduated from this book's self-service course.

Oh, did you not know this book doubled as an introductory School of Spankology? Well, surprise!

And, again, congratulations.

All of my best,

Clarine Klein

Clarine Klein, Professor of Spankology

CERTIFICATE OF COMPLETION

Clarine Klein's Self-Service School of Spankology

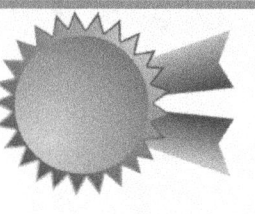

This Certificate is presented to:

_____
(Name Here)

For Successfully Completing:

Introduction to Spankology

Awarded on: _____ / _____ / _____

Answers to Frequently Asked Questions

As a Professor of Spankology, it is only natural that I receive many, many letters of correspondence from Caregivers seeking out my wisdom in the field, and in the interest of reducing the strain on the postal service, below are the answers to several of the questions I receive on a regular basis.

> **Where can I purchase one of the less ubiquitous Spanking Implements you recommend?**

Unfortunately, one cannot just pop down to the local hardware store and pick up a paddle or leather strap on their way home from work. That being said, Spanking Implements aren't nearly so hard to find out in the wild as you might think. For instance, any feed and tackle shop will have an abundance of readymade saddle straps for horses that just so happen to double exceptionally well as straps for bratty Littles and Middles. Moreover, you'd be amazed what you can find for sale in antique shops (I know I've certainly stumbled across several wonderful finds while out antiquing), and when all else fails the internet is your best friend. Etsy has a ton of great Spanking Implement vendors selling on it, and eBay is an excellent resource for those Caregivers looking for something a little more vintage in the vein of a razor strop or ebony hairbrush.

Should I be the one to bare my Little or Middle's bottom before their spanking?

There are two schools of thought among Spankologists regarding this particular question. The first camp believes that requiring your Little or Middle to bare their own bottom allows them to become an active participant in their punishment and establishes a humbling headspace that leads to more Effective Discipline, while others argue instead that baring your Little or Middle yourself sends a clear message to them that you, their Caregiver, are the one in charge and your rules are not to be ignored.

When you get right down to it, though, the answer is a resounding: Maybe.

I myself subscribe to the belief that Caregivers should be the one to bare a Little or Middle's bottom, as explained in the Preparing Your Little or Middle for Their Spanking subsection of the Giving a Spanking the Correct Way chapter of this book, but either approach is totally valid and whichever feels the most right to you is the one you should stick with.

Should I scold my Little or Middle while I'm spanking them?

Again, this is a topic that is hotly contested among Spankologists. However, it is this author's opinion that a Caregiver's primary lecturing should be reserved for directly before or after a spanking. Your Little or Middle is going to be plenty busy just enduring their spanking when it's actually happening, so there's no need to pile a conversation on top of that else as well!

Should I spank my Little or Middle in front of Others?

As was discussed in *Achieving Effective Discipline through Embarrassment*, Effective Discipline starts long before the first swat of a spanking is ever given, and Embarrassment is the foundation upon which all memorable and behavior-improving consequences are built. Bearing this in mind, spanking your Little or Middle in front of others is an excellent idea! Not only will it make your Little or Middle's spanking more memorable, but will also serve as an excellent object lesson for any other Littles or Middles who happen to be watching at the time.

So, yes, spank away in front of witnesses to your heart's content!

> **My Middle says they're too big to be spanked. What should I do?**

Wanton defiance and becoming "too big for your britches" are two extremely common occurrences of misbehavior among Middles. It is common and not something you should concern yourself with. However, if your Middle tells you they're too big for a spanking, you should immediately turn them over your knee and show them just how wrong they are before then requiring them to wear diapers or pull-ups for at least a week. Doing so is guaranteed to nip such nonsense right in the bud!

> **I had to give my Little or Middle multiple spankings in a single day! What am I doing wrong?**

So long as you are adhering to the teachings of this book, then you have nothing to worry about. Some Littles and Middles are simply more obstinate than others, especially if you are just starting to implement the techniques discussed in this book. Just be patient and continue to give them as many spankings as they need, and their behavior will eventually begin to improve. I promise.

REMEMBER!

SPANKING ISN'T THE ONLY TOOL IN YOUR DISCIPLINARY ARSENAL. A SUPPLEMENTARY PUNISHMENT CAN GO A LONG WAY TOWARD ACHIEVING EFFECTIVE DISCIPLINE, SO DON'T SKIMP ON THOSE!

> **I find myself having to give my Little or Middle a spanking for the same thing over and over again. What am I doing wrong?**

Much as many of my colleagues in the field of Spankology are loath to admit, even the most perfectly-executed Discipline Spanking and/or Supplementary Punishment isn't guaranteed to stop a particular act of misbehavior from occurring again. Just as one does not become too swole to control after a single workout at the gym, so too does a Little or Middle's misbehavior not completely disappear after one punishment.

That being said, if you find yourself having to repeat a spanking for the same misbehavior over and over again, chances are you're not making your Little or Middle's punishment embarrassing enough. As was discussed in *Achieving Effective Discipline through Embarrassment*, Effective Discipline starts long before the first swat of a spanking is ever given, and embarrassment is the foundation upon which all memorable and behavior-improving consequences are built.

So, make things more embarrassing! Instead of just giving your Little or Middle a spanking, bare their bottom and send them out to cut a couple switches, or maybe give them a spanking in The Diaper Position and then make them wear pull-ups for the next week. Your options are endless, so don't be afraid to get creative. Your little or Middle will thank you for it!

> **My Little or Middle's Bottom is too sore for a spanking! What should I do?**

Sometimes a spanking just can't be given right away, and that's all right. In such circumstances, a Little or Middle's spanking should be postponed until a time when their bottom is sufficiently recovered enough to be punished once again (such as at bedtime that evening, or right after breakfast the following morning). In the meantime, a Caregiver should implement at least one of the Supplementary Punishments outlined in Recommended Supplementary Punishments in order to ensure that their Little or Middle does not feel like they have gotten away with something they shouldn't have.

> **I find myself regretting the last punishment I gave my Little or Middle. Obviously this is irrational and silly, so what should I do?**

Nobody likes to be the bad guy, but that is unfortunately part and parcel of being a good Caregiver from time to time. However, just as you can't make an omelet without breaking a few eggs, so too can you not improve a Little or Middle's behavior without spanking a few butts! To that end, this author recommends that rather than dialing back your discipline when feelings of trepidation begin to crop up, you should instead increase the number of spankings you give your Little or Middle. Doing so will not only afford you both the opportunity to become more accustomed to them, and thus will alleviate any irrational feelings of regret on your part, but will also help to accelerate the improvement of your Little or Middle's behavior overall as well.

REMEMBER!

IF ONE SPANKING IS GOOD, THEN THREE IS EVEN BETTER!

My Little or Middle is so well-behaved. Do I really need to give them a Maintenance Spanking every week?

Yes, you absolutely do!

A Maintenance Spanking is not a punishment, and exactly how obedient or disobedient your particular Little or Middle is should have no bearing on whether or not they need one. Rather, Maintenance Spankings are an opportunity for you and your Little or Middle to sit down and review their behavior for the past week, as well as to nip any potential future misbehavior in the bud before it has a chance to take root.

REMEMBER!

JUST AS A STITCH IN TIME SAVES NINE, A SORE BOTTOM FOR YOUR LITTLE OR MIDDLE NOW WILL SAVE THEM FROM NEEDING A MORE SEVERE SPANKING IN THE FUTURE!

Thank you for reading!

If you enjoyed this book, please don't forget to leave a review, those help a lot.

Also, why not pick up another of my books while you're at it?

Getting spanked is a pain in the butt, but documenting it doesn't have to be!

From world-renowned Professor of Spankology Clarine Klein comes the spanking diary to end all spanking diaries. Based on her techniques from The Caregiver's Guide to Strict and Loving Discipline, this official spanking diary makes keeping a record of your Little or Middle's behavior easier than ever!

The Caregiver's Guide to Strict and Loving Discipline Spanking Diary Includes:

- A pre-prepared behavior contract for your Little or Middle
- 50 pre-prepared spanking report pages
- 30 pre-prepared spanking permission forms

Get yours today, available now from all major retailers!

More books by Clarine Klein

Back to Her Teens

A Lesbian Ageplay Spanking Romance

Petite and oh so sassy college sophomore Rhen Mathews is being kicked out of her dorms to make room for new students, and is in desperate need of a place to live. And so, when Dana Johnson, her former boss and burgeoning dommy-mommy girlfriend, offers to let her move in with her, she accepts without a second thought.

The only condition?

When in public, she has to pretend to be her thirteen-year-old niece from out of town.

What follows is a forced regression/ageplay romance novel filled to the brim with super embarrassing moments for Rhen and lots of much-needed spanking and discipline from her loving, but very strict, Auntie Dana.

Stuck in Her Teens

A Lesbian Ageplay Spanking Romance

Pretending to be her adoring (but super strict) mommy-dommy's niece while out in public has become just a normal part of life for petite and oh so sassy college junior Rhen Mathews. With her small frame and bratty attitude, it's not exactly a hard fit, and she knows that when she gets out of line she can expect to find herself being taken across her partner's lap for a good old-fashioned bare bottom spanking.

But, what happens when her "aunt" starts giving others permission to discipline her?

Surely that nice old lady from down the street or her best friend from the dorms wouldn't *actually* spank her, would they?

Well, as her partner is fond of saying: "If the panties fit, they might as well come down for a spanking!"

What follows is a forced regression/ageplay romance novel filled to the brim with super embarrassing moments for Rhen and lots of much-needed spanking and discipline from her loving, but very strict, Auntie Dana.

MELODY HARPER
SUBMISSIVE OF DARKNESS

CLARINE KLEIN

Melody Harper, Submissive of Darkness

A Werewolf and Vampire Spanking Romance Novel

What happens when a bratty vampire bites off more than she can chew?

College freshman and recently-turned vampire, Melody Harper, is trying to live her best unlife. Fresh out of the closet and eager to make up for lost time, she goes hunting for a date / midnight snack at the local girl bar just off campus. Only problem is, the muscular butch she's set her sights on turns out to be a werewolf Alpha who doesn't take too kindly to involuntary blood donations.

Morgan Bloodfang can't believe her luck when the most adorable baby goth she's ever seen starts flirting with her while she's out drinking one night. Plump in all the right places and with a submissive streak a mile wide, she's just her type. Only problem is, her shy dance partner turns out to have eyes bigger than her stomach when she passes out on top of her after going for her jugular.

Escorting the unconscious girl home, Morgan fully intends on giving her a piece of her mind (and a dose of her belt) once she wakes up, only to end up claiming her as her mate instead. It might be sudden, but instinct has never led her astray before, and she doubts it will now. Only problem is, Melody is a gigantic brat, and if they're going to make things work, she's going to have to learn her place.

Over her Alpha's knee.

Blazing Tales of the Blazar Bitches

A Spanking Space Pirate Adventure

Being a pirate is hard when you're the one with all the booty!

For Phera Sinclair, life aboard a remote asteroid mining facility is nice and predictable. Sure, she might be a corporate slave working to pay back student loans that will never actually go away, but at least she has a job, right?

That all changes when she's caught up in a shipjacking by the Blazar Bitches!

After an explosive (and erotically-charged) first encounter with the gruff and frustratingly attractive space pirate, Straya, Phera finds herself being press-ganged into the crew. Free of the chains of her old life, she's able to use her PhD in robotics to help rob megacorporations blind in between learning firsthand just what being a horny brat among a crew of spank-happy space pirates means for her and her way too jiggly backside in this hard sci-fi adventure with even harder spankings!

Cat and Mouse

Clarine Klein

Cat and Mouse

A Lesbian Romance Spanking Novella

Cassidy Coleman is a sassy but introverted college sophomore out on her own for the first time in her young adult life. At the start of fall semester, she moves into an apartment with a randomly assigned roommate, Lauren Delaney. Lauren is a an outgoing and athletic economics major one year ahead of Cassidy in school, and is just looking for a place to live that doesn't also double up as a party house on the weekends.

Unfortunately, things start off more than a little awkward between the two of them at first, with Cassidy too tongue-tied by the captivating older girl to carry on more than a two sentence conversation before needing to flee to her bedroom. Eventually though, the two manage to bond over a mutual love of video games from their childhood, and overnight an instant and lifelong friendship is forged. From there friendship then blossoms into love when after pushing her roommate into a freezing pool on a chilly winter night, Cassidy suddenly finds herself being hauled across Lauren's ample lap for a bare bottom blistering they've both been dreaming of for weeks.

And it's only the beginning!

The Water Nymph's Plaything

Clarine Klein
Leila Hann

The Water Nymph's Plaything

A Lesbian Spanking Fantasy Adventure

Fresh from her novice training as a sister of the Celestine Order, Sally Vinebrook travels the world in search of magical secrets to further her education in the arcane arts. Following up on a rumor, she comes across The Misty Bog, home to an ancient and powerful water nymph named Modan.

After begging for a chance to study with her for a time, and a very thorough spanking for being so disrespectful to her swamp upon arrival, she is shown a brand new world of magic unlike anything she's ever known!

Though by the end of her stay, she just might not be able to sit down ever again.